M000007351

GRILLIN' LIKE A VILLAIN

0 11557 03325 0

GRILLIN' LIKE A VILLAIN

The Complete Grilling and Barbecuing Cookbook

Rick Black

STACKPOLE
BOOKS

Copyright © 2006 by Stackpole Books

Published by
STACKPOLE BOOKS
5067 Ritter Road
Mechanicsburg, PA 17055
www.stackpolebooks.com

All rights reserved, including the right to reproduce this book or portions
thereof in any form or by any means, electronic or mechanical, including
photocopying, recording, or by any information storage and retrieval system,
without permission in writing from the publisher. All inquiries should be
addressed to Stackpole Books, 5067 Ritter Road, Mechanicsburg,
Pennsylvania 17055.

Printed in the United States

First edition

10 9 8 7 6 5 4 3 2 1

Cover design by Wendy A. Reynolds
Cover illustration by Daniel Roberts

Library of Congress Cataloging-in-Publication Data
Black, Rick.
   Grillin' like a villain : the complete grilling and barbecuing cookbook / Rick
Black.— 1st ed.
      p. cm.
   Includes index.
   ISBN-13: 978-0-8117-3325-0 (alk. paper)
   ISBN-10: 0-8117-3325-4 (alk. paper)
   1. Barbecue cookery. I. Title.

TX840.B3B556 2006
641.5'784—dc22
                                                                    2006003655

To my little brother Mike Black.

From the time we were kids riding our bikes pretending we were CHiPS, Mike has always wanted to be a police officer.

Mike earned his way through college and was a deputy sheriff at the age of twenty-two.

One year later he became the police chief of a new department, and three years after that, a proud state trooper in Florida. Mike, his wife April, and daughter Alyssa still reside in the state he protects. Without a doubt, "To Serve and Protect" is a motto that Mike and the fellow troopers of his post live by.

CONTENTS

ACKNOWLEDGMENTS

My thanks for help in furnishing data, photos, and for sharing their time, knowledge, and experience go to Mike Hoffman of Keystone; Brad Holland of the Holland Grill Company; Dan Roberts, my cartoonist; Cosmo of The New Mix 107.3 radio show; Judith Schnell of Stackpole Books; Terry Lee for my computer support; the Food Guru Chef Peter Harman; Fareway Stores; the staff and crew of Martini's Grille for letting me play with their cool stuff; Fleck Sales (the beer boys); Farm King Supply Stores; Robin Delaney of the *Fort Madison Democrat*; the *Keokuk Daily Gate City*; Cris Roberts of the *Burlington Hawkeye*; and thanks to the remaining media folks for making this hillbilly look good. And as always a special note of thanks also to Amy Lerner for editing the manuscript through all its convolutions with patience and insight and gentle firmness.

Finally, I am ever so grateful for the ongoing love and support of my family—Becky, Shaena, and Travis—from whom I've stolen time to work on this project.

R. B.

INTRODUCTION

"Grillin' like a villain." Those are the words you would likely hear from your old cousin Rick if you were to call on any given summer's day. Shoot, you might as well include the spring and fall months too!

Despite the thousands of meals I have prepared on a grill, I still get a thrill from smelling the coals or watching blue flames escape the burner holes of a deluxe outdoor range. I have had the privilege of grillin' in just about every one of our United States with some of the best outdoor chefs. From Fort Worth, Texas, to St. Louis, Missouri, from Kansas City to Green Bay, Wisconsin, and all places in between, barbecuing is and has been an art that is almost a religion.

The pros will tell you that grilling is not barbecuing. They will tell you that grilling is cooking over direct heat like what you get from a gas grill, whereas barbecuing is cooking by using indirect heat at low temperatures and slow cooking times like what you get from coals. No matter what type of cooking method you prefer, the various seasonings and their methods, wet rubs, dry rubs, sauces, and marinades, produce the different flavors of your meal.

I will cover all types of grilling and barbecuing techniques and recipes in this book, but before we get started on the recipes, there are a few rules that you must first learn before you're out there slapping burgers in the wind. I will call them Cousin Rick's 11 Rules of Barbecuing.

1. **Grill ready.** Have everything you need ready for grilling: the food, marinade, basting sauce, seasonings, and equipment on hand and at the grill before you start.

2. **Don't tucker out.** I can't think of anything worse than running out of gas or charcoal in the middle of grillin'! When using charcoal, light enough to form a bed of glowing coals four inches larger on all sides than the surface area of the food you're planning to cook. When cooking on a gas grill, make sure the tank is at least one-third full. Remember to check your tanks often. I always have a spare tank ready.

3. **Heat it up.** Remember, grilling is a high-heat cooking method. In order to achieve the seared crust, charcoal flavor, and distinct grill marks associated with masterpiece grilling, you must cook over high heat. How high you ask? At least 500 degrees. When using charcoal, let it burn until it is covered with a thin coat of gray ash. When using a gas grill, preheat to high (at least 500 degrees); this takes about fifteen minutes. When indirect grilling, try to preheat the grill to 350 degrees.

4. **Cleanliness is next to grilliness.** There's nothing less appetizing than grilling on dirty old bits of burnt food stuck to the grate! Besides, the food will stick to a dirty grate. Clean the grate twice: once after you've preheated the grill and again when you've finished cooking. The first cleaning will remove any bits of food you may have missed after your last grilling adventure. Use the edge of a metal spatula to scrape off large bits of food; I use a stiff wire brush to finish scrubbing the grate.

5. **Don't let it stick.** Oil the grate just before placing the food on it. If necessary, spray it with oil (away from the flames), use a folded paper towel soaked in vegetable oil, or rub it with a piece of fatty bacon, beef fat, or fatty chicken skin. How's that for a great flavor tip!

6. **Don't be a Michael Myers.** The proper way to turn meat on a grill is with tongs or a spatula. Never stab the meat with a carving fork unless you want to drain the flavor-rich juices onto the coals. Save your fork for the salad!

7. **Don't waste the baste.** Oil-and-vinegar-, citrus-, and yogurt-based bastes and marinades can be brushed on the meat throughout the cooking time. (If you baste with a marinade that you used for raw meat or seafood, do not apply it dur-

ing the last three minutes of cooking.) When using a sugar-based barbecue sauce, apply it toward the end of the cooking time. The sugar in these sauces burns easily and should not be exposed to prolonged heat.

8. **Keep your meat undercover.** When cooking larger cuts of meat and poultry, such as whole chicken, leg of lamb, or prime rib, use an indirect method of grilling or barbecuing. Keep the grill tightly covered and resist the temptation to peek. Every time you lift the lid, you add five to ten minutes to the cooking time.

9. **Rest assured.** Beef, steak, and chicken, in fact almost anything you grill, will taste better if you let it stand on the cutting board for a few minutes before serving. This allows the meat juices, which have been driven to the center of the roast or steak by the searing heat, to return to the surface. The result is a juicier, tastier piece of meat.

10. **Atten hut!** Grilling is an easy cooking method, but it demands constant attention. Once you put something on the grill (especially when using the direct fire method), stay with it until it's cooked. Have a helper grab a cold one if you need it; you're the grill boss, manage your project.

11. **Have a blast with the cast.** Above all, have fun. When you're the grill master, you are the director of the crowd you are serving. Grilling is one of the most enjoyable means of cooking; enjoy yourself and get everyone involved, especially the young. The art of barbecuing has been passed down many generations and cultures. It's part of our history!

If you're going to teach the art of barbecuing, you might want to know a little history on the subject. Many folks state that the word *barbecue* actually comes from the French phrase "barbe a queue," meaning "from head to tail."

Some will argue that the word *barbecue* came from migrants from the Caribbean who ended up in South Carolina. However the term barbecue came to us, one thing is certain: We can directly relate it to the southern United States through pork or what is better known as a hog roast. Pork was a major meat in the southern states of Alabama, Georgia, Louisiana, Mississippi, Missouri, North Carolina,

South Carolina, and Tennessee. These southern states pride themselves on outstanding pork barbecuing. Don't worry, Virginia, I'm going to save you for later!

So what do the other southern states, such as Texas and Oklahoma, barbecue? Well, most likely the answer is beef. I have several friends in the South, and they always poke fun at me for being an Iowa native by saying we in the North call barbecuing "cookouts." That's true, I reply, but I have had to learn how to grill it all—chicken, beef, lamb, pork, and seafood. And that includes all the rubs, brines, sauces, and marinades too.

I think the word *barbecue* is misused. When you cook steaks, hot dogs, and hamburgers (and whatever else you want) on the grill, that is called grilling. Cooking meat over an open fire has been around since the cave man days. But the cave man didn't barbecue. Why? Because he had no sauce! So just what is barbecuing? To barbecue is to slow-cook meat at a low temperature for a long time over wood or charcoal, not gas, although most backyard grillin' bandits without culinary palettes don't know the difference.

The basic barbecue grill is a cooking chamber with an offset firebox or a water smoker. The average gas grill is not meant for barbecuing but for grilling.

Barbecuing began in the late 1800s during cattle drives out West. The cowboys had to be fed and the boss didn't want to feed them the good meat, so other disposable cuts were used to feed the men. The main choice was the brisket, which is a very tough, stringy piece of meat. However, the cowboys learned that if they left this brisket cooking for a long time (five to seven hours) at approximately 200 degrees, they had a great-tasting meal. Besides brisket, other meats they found that barbecued well were pork butt, pork ribs, beef ribs, venison, and goat.

Digging a pit (to concentrate cooking heat and smoke) comes from our European heritage, but it was forgotten until the Jamestown colonists arrived. Since pigs were running around freely, pork became the sustenance meat of Virginia and later the southern states. This also was a blessing when crops didn't produce.

Texas seems to love beef barbecue, which again only seems logical due to all the cattle in the region. And it's my own personal experience that the West coast, especially Californians, seem to love chicken or seafood grilling.

Barbecuing tastes and cooking methods differ, but one thing that's undeniable is that barbecuing is popular and well-loved in American society. I have had the privilege of barbecuing with the best chefs from all over the country and elsewhere—I even got great grillin' recipes from Jamaica, such as jerked pork and chicken. Purists claim that a grilled piece of meat slapped with some sauce after cooking isn't real barbecue at all. Others say it is, as long as the sauce is there. I say the secret to good barbecue cooking is in the heat or a good bed of coals. The secret to a successful barbecue cookout is in the sauce.

First the heat: It's best to place your cooking grill about five inches above the coals. This is recommended for good thorough cooking. Shish kebabs will be done in twenty to thirty minutes, hamburgers in eight to ten minutes, and larger pieces of meat should be done in about twenty minutes per pound. Whatever sauce is used, one like I will cover in this book or one purchased from the grocery store, you should apply it lavishly while the meat is cooking. And make darn sure more sauce is available when it's time to serve the meat!

Grills fall into two broad categories: charcoal fired and gas. Let's learn about these types of grills.

CHARCOAL GRILLS

Charcoal grills are subdivided into those that are open and those that are closed (virtually all gas grills have lids). Open grills are simply grates over glowing embers that are nestled in a trough of some kind.

The hibachi grill is the most elemental of open grills, and anyone who has been cramped for space or money (or both, if you were like me in college) has probably had this Japanese-style grill at one time. Its low-to-the-ground, rectangular shape takes up little room, and it costs next to nothing at hardware or discount stores. Though limited in size and temperature control, hibachis are quite serviceable for grilling small items such as hamburgers or chicken breasts. I have eaten many deer loins cooked on hibachi grills at camps. They are fast and easily stored in a cabin.

Other open grills are essentially souped-up versions of hibachis. For example, the grill surface may be larger to accommodate a whole salmon, and the grate may be elevated or lowered several settings to regulate the intensity of the heat on the food. A larger grill also offers you the flexibility of moving food around, so cooked food can be transferred to a cooler spot on the grill and food not yet cooked shifted to a hotter spot.

Covered grills such as the popular kettle grills can cook food by direct heat, though the grill height is usually not adjustable. To compensate, heat is diffused by the dome design and adjusted by controlling the air flow from vents in the top and bottom of the closed kettle. Kettle grills can, of course, be used as open grills too. But kettle grills can also cook foods such as whole turkeys with indirect heat in barbecue-type fashion. I say barbecue-type because it's not really grilling over direct, intense heat, nor is it genuine barbecue.

GAS GRILLS

Gas grills, which now account for the vast majority of grill sales, are cleaner, but purists think they don't give the real grilled flavor that charcoal-fired grills do. That may depend on the keenness of your taste buds, but there's no getting around the fact that charcoal grills are messier, and you've always got to remember to bring the charcoal and a match.

With gas grills, the most important element is the burner because it wears out first. Cast iron is the preferred material, but brass is even better. Porcelain or enamel-coated cast iron grates are also recommended because they conduct heat better and sear more effectively. They also heat up faster and are easier to clean.

TOOLS OF THE TRADE

The following is a list of recommended grilling tools. Nothing is worse than being a guest at a barbecue and witnessing the cook grab a rack of ribs using a pair of needle-nose pliers because he doesn't have the correct grilling tools. Rookies!

Long-handled tongs and spatulas. Used to turn food on the grill. Preferred over long-handled forks to prevent piercing of meats, the long handles keep your hands and arms safe from the heat.

Long-handled basting brush. A brush specifically made to apply marinades and barbecue sauce a safe distance from intense grill heat. A smaller-handled brush is appropriate for applying a thin coat of oil to grill grates (before the grill is started) to keep the foods from sticking.

Oven mitts. Protect hands and lower arms from the heat. Mitts for grilling are longer to protect more of the arm. Two alternatives are silicone and welding gloves. I have found that both have a resistance to high heat and protect the lower arm from burns.

Meat thermometer. Instant-read thermometers work best when grilling. Thermometers with an extended tip are made specifically for grilling to protect the cook from heat. Testing meat with a thermometer is the only way to guarantee the meat is done and safe to serve.

Wire grill brush/grate cleaner. This is a stiff metal brush specifically used for cleaning the grill grate. The grill brush is most effective if used soon after the grill has been used and the grate is still hot. Wire grill brushes and grate cleaners are available in many different styles. I have over twelve different types.

Drip pans. I use drip pans to protect from fire flareups, and they make cleanup a whole heap easier when grilling with indirect heat. They are essential if you're using a rotisserie.

Water spray bottle. I use this to extinguish flareups from food dripping on the coals. I recommend this for charcoal grills only.

Barbecue hook. The barbecue hook is a great option for grillers for turning meat on the grill. This tool hooks into the meat so you can securely flip it over while preventing accidental drops. (A lifesaver if the cook has been kicking back a few frosty ones.)

Skewers/skewer holder. These tools are available in metal and bamboo. I would recommend that you soak the bamboo skewers for about thirty minutes before placing them on the grill to ensure they will not burn. Skewer holders keep the skewers raised up off of the grate, preventing burning of the kebabs.

Fish basket. This is a true party saver. This type of basket is made to hold the fish securely as it cooks, making it easy to flip and preventing it from falling apart on the grill. Buy the type that is contoured in the shape of a fish.

Wire grill basket. Essential when grilling small pieces of food that cannot be placed directly on the grate or won't stay on skewers. The convenience of a basket is the ability to flip food without using any additional tools. Used for meat, fish, fruits, and vegetables. Long-handled wire baskets are the perfect tool when cooking directly over an open fire.

Grill screen. This little tool is a screen that is placed directly on the grill grate to prevent small foods from falling through onto the coals.

Roasting rack. This gadget is a rack for keeping large cuts of meat from touching the grates. The rack makes removal, rotating, and cleanup faster and easier. I use this tool most often with chicken and turkey.

Flavor injector. A must have! My favorite sauces and marinades are at your fingertips in this great book. Take advantage of this and use a flavor injector. It is easy; inject the sauce into any type of food for more flavor and texture.

Charcoal electric starter. You can always tell who the pros are by the tools they use when grilling. The electric starter is for charcoal grills only. Attached to a heavy-duty extension cord, this metal looped starter is placed into the center pyramid of charcoal. Within ten to fifteen minutes the coals should be red hot; the starter is then removed and set in a safe place to cool down.

Long-handled butane lighter. These multi-purpose lighters keep your hands safely away from direct contact when starting a grill fire. We have several, and my wife uses them for lighting candles, outdoor torches, and such.

Rotisserie. This tool is used for slow, indirect, even cooking of meat. Rotisserie cooking uses less heat because the grill lid stays shut. My rotisserie is motorized and rotates the meat constantly until it is done. Coals should be built around the edges of the grill and a drip pan placed directly under the meat.

Chimney starter. This is a large, hollow, upright cylinder used to ignite charcoal evenly. The cylinder is separated by a wire partition. You place crumpled newspaper below the wire partition and charcoal on top. Light the paper on the bottom, and in about thirty minutes the charcoal is glowing orange-red.

In these brief pages we have covered history, types of barbecuing and grilling, tools of the trade. . . . So what are we missing? Yes! How to host a barbecue? It can be done in eight easy steps.

1. **What's up?** Always send your invitations a couple of weeks in advance. Remember that summertime grilling events are

common. Let your guests know the date, time, and what to bring, if anything, well in advance.

2. **Have a plan, Stan.** Planning your menu and letting your guests know what's being served in advance is a great way for them to know how to dress and what to bring. Decide what types of marinades and sauces you will be making in advance along with the cuts of meat you wish to cook.

3. **Washing it down.** Plan your drinks. If it's hot, have plenty of cold drinks. Remember to have nonalcoholic drinks, such as soda, water, and tea, available, in addition to beer and such for the party crowd. A good host will keep an eye on his guests. Be ready to call a cab or have a plan to drive your boozehounds home.

4. **Snack attack.** I recommend that you prepare some snacks for the guests to eat while they are waiting for the main meal. Something easy and light like homemade chips works great.

5. **Ready Freddie.** When you receive your RSVPs, take count and make sure you have ample party supplies—plates, cups, napkins, utensils—place them where they're easily accessible. Remember, this is a barbecue, so have plenty of paper towels available.

6. **Sit on it.** Ever been to a barbecue and had to stand while you ate because there weren't enough tables and chairs? Although my publisher likes my books to be rated PG-13, I gotta tell ya, this sucks! Always have plenty of tables and chairs for your guests. Remember to have tables ready for the food also. Place the food tables away from the grill; we don't need any little helpers getting burned while the adults are eating and talking.

7. **Is it time to eat?** When planning your grilling event, remember to allow grilling time for the food. If you're planning on serving at 6 P.M., make sure you're ready by 3 P.M. Remember that your marinading should already be done, and allow thirty minutes for your coals if using charcoal.

8. **Something for everyone.** Always have party games at your event. If it's in your backyard, try volleyball or badminton. If your event is in a park, try horseshoes or softball. Frisbee

golf has been a big hit for my family during the past couple of years. Break off into groups and have the adults play the kids or families play each other. Have fun! If you're having a family reunion, T-shirts with the date and family tree are a must-have! If it's a neighborhood gathering, T-shirts with street or neighborhood names would be good.

There is no end to barbecue and grilling cookbooks. And yet for this particular one there is, it seems to me, a very real need because of the constantly growing number of those who have heretofore enjoyed meals prepared by good professional barbecue cooks and who now find they neither are economically able to pay the high wages that even an average barbecue cook commands today (if indeed they can secure one at all) nor can afford to dine regularly in expensive barbecue restaurants. There is only one solution for those who want really good barbecue food: Learn to cook it yourself.

It is for those who appreciate and long for really good barbecue food that this book has been written. Its aim is to make it possible for even the inexperienced to prepare the delicious barbecue dishes that otherwise would generally be unavailable. This book will do just that and more! I fully intend for this book to not only make your life at the grill a fun-filled event, but to put a few smiles on your face as you read it.

Enjoy!

CHAPTER ONE

GRILLIN' RUBS

The key to a great barbecue starts with the rubs. Grillin' rubs come wet and dry. I will start this chapter with the dry rubs and then move on to the wet rubs, but before I do that, let me tell you just what a rub is.

A rub is a mixture of herbs, spices, and seasonings liberally applied to coat the outside of the meat you're going to grill. Salt is always a great starting place for a rub. Salt helps the rub penetrate, and it rounds out and brings together the flavors of the ingredients. Sugar is also a popular addition to rubs as it caramelizes when exposed to high heat.

The one thing to keep in mind when using my rub recipes is that you can add or subtract any of the ingredients to your liking. Rubs are about the flavor you desire. So get ready to have some fun!

DRY RUBS

Fort Worth BBQ Rub

3 tablespoons brown sugar
2 tablespoons paprika
2 tablespoons dry mustard
2 tablespoons onion powder
2 tablespoons garlic powder
2 tablespoons dried sweet basil
$^1/_2$ tablespoon minced bay leaves
$^1/_2$ tablespoon coriander
$^1/_2$ tablespoon ground savory
$^1/_2$ tablespoon ground thyme
$^1/_2$ tablespoon black pepper
2 teaspoons sea salt
$^1/_2$ teaspoon ground cumin

In a large mixing bowl, mix all the ingredients together. Rub into the meat at least 4 hours before grilling.

Sidewinder Rub

$^1/_4$ cup paprika
2 tablespoons salt
2 tablespoons onion powder
2 tablespoons garlic powder
2 tablespoon black pepper
2 tablespoons cayenne pepper
2 tablespoons white pepper
I tablespoon sugar

In a large mixing bowl, mix all the ingredients together, and rub into the meat at least 4 hours before grilling.

Porgy's Revenge

8 tablespoons salt
8 tablespoons sugar
8 tablespoons brown sugar
8 tablespoons ground cumin
8 tablespoons chili powder
8 tablespoons ground black pepper
5 tablespoons cayenne pepper
18 tablespoons paprika

In a large mixing bowl, combine all the ingredients together, and rub into a pork butt at least 12 hours before grilling.

Makayla's Carolina Pride

4 tablespoons paprika
1 tablespoon onion powder
1 tablespoon ground basil
2 tablespoons dry mustard
1 tablespoon red pepper
1 tablespoon ground black pepper

In a large mixing bowl, combine all the ingredients together, and rub into ribs 15 minutes before grilling.

Terry Lee's Navy Seal's Baby Back Rub

2 tablespoons ground cumin
2 tablespoons ground thyme
2 tablespoons sea salt
2 tablespoons freshly ground black pepper
1 teaspoon garlic powder

Mix all the ingredients. Apply the rub liberally to both sides of ribs.

Tyler Cook's BBQ Dry Rub

3 tablespoons chili powder

1 tablespoon paprika

2 tablespoons dried oregano

2 teaspoons garlic powder

1 teaspoon cayenne powder

1 teaspoon black pepper

1 teaspoon sugar

1 teaspoon dry mustard

1 teaspoon ground cloves

$1/2$ teaspoon ground thyme

$1/2$ teaspoon ground tarragon

$1/2$ teaspoon ground celery seed

$1/2$ teaspoon salt

Mix all the ingredients together well. Sprinkle over meat and rub well; cook with mesquite.

Pulaski Steak Rub

6 tablespoons dry mustard

4 tablespoons dried oregano

2 tablespoons chili powder

1 tablespoon garlic powder

1 tablespoon smoked salt

Mix all the ingredients together. Pat onto both sides of steak and grill.

Major Hayman's Porterhouse Rub

6 fresh garlic cloves, minced
1 teaspoon sea salt
1 teaspoon fresh ground black pepper
1 teaspoon ground oregano

Combine all ingredients. Mix until well blended. Rub evenly over the surface of porterhouse at least 30 minutes before grilling.

Chuck Wagon Roast Rub

2 teaspoons dried oregano
2 teaspoons dried thyme
2 teaspoons paprika
2 teaspoons salt
1 teaspoon garlic powder
1 teaspoon onion powder
1 teaspoon white pepper
1 teaspoon black pepper
$1/2$ teaspoon ground red pepper

Combine all the ingredients, and mix well. Rub evenly over the surface of your beef or pork roast at least 30 minutes before grilling.

Cousin Rick's Family Secret Hog Rub

6 tablespoons paprika
2 tablespoons onion powder
2 tablespoons garlic powder
3 tablespoons garlic salt
2 tablespoons smoked salt
2 tablespoons black pepper
2 tablespoons sugar
2 tablespoons dried ground basil
2 tablespoons dried ground oregano
2 tablespoons ground thyme
1 teaspoon sage
1 teaspoon dried ground nutmeg
1 teaspoon dried ground ginger
1 teaspoon cumin
1 teaspoon dried ground rosemary
1 teaspoon dry mustard
1 cup minced mint leaves
1/2 cup brown sugar
1/4 cup Accent

In a large bowl, mix all the ingredients together very well. Rub into hog on all sides at least 12 hours before grilling.

Holy Smokes Rub

8 tablespoons brown sugar
2 tablespoons garlic salt
1 tablespoon ground dried chilies
1 tablespoon ground black pepper
1 tablespoon cayenne
1 tablespoon paprika
1 tablespoon granulated garlic
1 tablespoon onion powder

Mix all the ingredients together, and rub into your choice of meat at least 20 minutes before grilling.

T-Bone Brown's Steak Rub

4 tablespoons salt

2 tablespoons paprika

I tablespoon ground black pepper

2 teaspoons onion powder

2 teaspoons garlic powder

2 teaspoons cayenne pepper

$1/2$ teaspoon turmeric

$1/2$ teaspoon coriander

Mix together, and rub into steaks at least 30 minutes before grilling.

Waterman's "Get Me a Beer!" Rub

I cup paprika

$1/2$ cup white pepper

$1/2$ cup brown sugar

6 tablespoons salt

6 tablespoons chili powder

4 tablespoons garlic powder

4 tablespoons onion powder

2 tablespoons cayenne

Mix all ingredients thoroughly, and rub into your favorite grilling meats. This rub works great with pork, beef, and lamb.

Old Bob Mabes' Dry Rib Rub

8 tablespoons garlic salt
8 tablespoons brown sugar
3 tablespoons freshly ground black pepper
2 tablespoons MSG
1 1/2 tablespoons lemon powder
1 1/2 tablespoons paprika

Combine all the ingredients together, and rub into all sides of your favorite choice of ribs at least 30 minutes before grilling.

Pammy Garr's Yard Bird Rub

8 tablespoons salt
3 tablespoons white pepper
2 tablespoons MSG
3 tablespoons garlic powder
1 tablespoon ground bay leaves
2 tablespoons dry mustard
2 tablespoons paprika

Mix all the ingredients together and rub into all sides of the chicken at least 15 minutes before grilling. This recipe will cover about three chickens. Double recipe if grilling more than five birds at once.

Gerry and Rose's Turkey Breast Grillin' Rub

4 tablespoons ground ginger
4 tablespoons sugar
4 tablespoons zest of orange
2 teaspoons white pepper
$^{1}/_{2}$ teaspoon ground nutmeg
$^{1}/_{2}$ teaspoon ground clove
$^{1}/_{2}$ teaspoon Accent

Combine all ingredients, and rub into turkey breast at least 15 minutes before grilling.

"Oh Momma It Burns" Rub

I tablespoon minced habanero peppers
I tablespoon minced ancho peppers
I tablespoon minced chipotle seeds
$^{1}/_{2}$ cup dried and minced tomatoes
I tablespoon garlic powder
I tablespoon smoked salt
I tablespoon white pepper
I teaspoon savory
I teaspoon Accent

Mix all the ingredients together, and rub into large chicken or turkey legs and wings at least 30 minutes before grilling. Note: This is not a recipe for sissies. Wash your hands immediately before touching your wife, girlfriend, or both!

Parrot Head Fish Rub

2 tablespoons ground cumin
2 tablespoons ground ginger
2 tablespoons Accent
2 tablespoons ground coriander
1 tablespoon paprika
1 tablespoon turmeric
1 tablespoon sea salt
1 tablespoon cayenne

Mix all the ingredients together, and rub into all sides of your favorite fish at least 15 minutes before grilling.

Charleston Pork Roast Rub

$1/4$ cup paprika
2 tablespoons onion salt
3 teaspoons dried oregano
1 tablespoon garlic powder
1 tablespoon dried thyme
1 teaspoon ground red pepper
$1/2$ teaspoon white pepper

Mix all the ingredients together, and rub into pork roast or ribs at least 1 hour before grilling.

Weaver Lamb Rub

6 tablespoons dry mustard
4 tablespoons dried oregano
3 tablespoons chili powder
1 tablespoon garlic salt
1 tablespoon onion salt
1 tablespoon white pepper

Mix all the ingredients together, and rub into your favorite cut of lamb at least 15 minutes before grilling.

Thunderstorm Sparerib Rub

1 cup brown sugar
$^1/_2$ cup paprika
2 tablespoons garlic salt
2 tablespoons freshly ground black pepper
1 tablespoon cayenne pepper
1 tablespoon onion powder

Mix all the ingredients together, and rub into all sides of the spareribs at least 30 minutes before grilling.

Hawkeye Tailgating Rub

2 tablespoons smoked salt
1 tablespoon garlic powder
1 tablespoon onion powder
1 teaspoon ground thyme
1 teaspoon sage
1 teaspoon paprika
1 teaspoon black pepper
1 teaspoon ground rosemary
1 teaspoon tarragon
1 teaspoon ground basil

Mix all the ingredients together, and store in an airtight container. When ready for tailgating, rub into all sides of your favorite meats at least 30 minutes before grilling. Go Hawks!

Smakin's New Orleans Prime Rib Rub

$1/4$ cup white pepper

2 tablespoons cinnamon

3 tablespoons garlic salt

2 tablespoons freshly ground black pepper

2 teaspoons ground thyme

2 teaspoons dried minced garlic

1 teaspoon onion powder

Mix all the ingredients together, and rub into all sides of the prime rib meat at least 1 hour before grilling.

Foghorn Leghorn Rub

$1/2$ cup paprika

$1/4$ cup celery salt

$1/4$ cup white pepper

$1/2$ cup sugar

3 tablespoons onion powder

2 tablespoons dry mustard

3 tablespoons cayenne powder

4 tablespoons lemon zest

Mix all the ingredients together, and rub into your choice of poultry at least 15 minutes before grilling.

Sweet Home Alabama Pulled Pork Rub

3 cups paprika
1 cup lemon pepper
1/2 cup freshly ground black pepper
1/4 cup onion salt
1/2 cup dried minced garlic
1/2 cup chili powder
1 cup brown sugar
1/4 cup Accent

Mix all the ingredients together, and rub into hog meat at least 30 minutes before grilling.

Ocho Rios Jerk Pork or Chicken Rub

It took me six days to finally talk this recipe out of chef Mickey, but it was well worth it! This is true Jamaican barbecuing.

1/2 cup onion powder
1/2 cup garlic powder
4 tablespoons allspice
4 tablespoons brown sugar
2 tablespoons ground chipotle
2 tablespoons ground thyme
2 tablespoons cinnamon
3 tablespoons lemon zest
1 teaspoon nutmeg
1 teaspoon chili powder
1 teaspoon sea salt

Combine all the ingredients together, and rub into pork or chicken 30 minutes before grilling.

Too hot? No problem, mon, adjust it to your liking.

BBQ Bert's All-Purpose Pork Rub

4 tablespoons paprika
2 tablespoons salt
4 tablespoons brown sugar
2 tablespoons ground cumin
2 tablespoons chili powder
2 tablespoons black pepper
I tablespoon cayenne pepper

Mix all the ingredients together, and rub into pork at least 15 minutes before grilling.

Billy's Beef Brisket Rub

8 tablespoons chili powder
I teaspoon cayenne pepper
3 teaspoons black pepper
5 teaspoons garlic powder

Mix all the ingredients together, and rub into beef briskets at least 30 minutes before grilling.

Indian Lake Whole Hog Rub

2 cups ground black pepper
2 cups chili powder
2 cups sugar
I cup garlic salt
6 tablespoons dry mustard
6 tablespoons cayenne
4 tablespoons Accent

Mix all the ingredients together, and rub into all sides of hog meat at least 30 minutes before grilling.

Fripp Island Carolina Hog Rub

2 cups red chili powder

3 tablespoons paprika

8 tablespoons cumin

4 tablespoons minced cloves

1 tablespoon ground fenugreek

1 tablespoon sea salt

1 teaspoon ground cardamom

1 tablespoon ground black pepper

1 tablespoon ground coriander

1 teaspoon ground ginger

1 teaspoon allspice

$^1/_2$ teaspoon turmeric

$^1/_2$ teaspoon cinnamon

Combine all the ingredients together, and rub into all sides of pork at least 1 hour before grilling or smoking.

Mike and April's Pensacola Poultry Rub

2 tablespoons garlic powder

4 teaspoons seasoned salt

2 teaspoons poultry seasoning

2 teaspoons paprika

2 teaspoons sea salt

1 teaspoon pepper

$^1/_2$ teaspoon cayenne pepper

$^1/_2$ teaspoon dried basil

Combine all the ingredients together, and rub into turkey or chicken at least 20 minutes before grilling. Remember to always get rub ingredients under the skin to seal in the great flavors of this recipe.

Cajun Joe's Momma's Rub

$1/2$ cup paprika
5 tablespoons salt
$1/4$ cup black pepper
4 tablespoons dried basil
4 tablespoons garlic powder
2 tablespoons onion powder
3 tablespoons cayenne pepper
2 tablespoons dried oregano
2 tablespoons white pepper
1 tablespoon Accent
1 tablespoon dried thyme

Mix all the ingredients together, and rub into your favorite meat that you wish to grill Cajun-style.

When your guests ask where you got this great-tasting recipe, quickly answer back, "Joe Momma!"

Travis's Veggie Rub

1 tablespoon salt
1 tablespoon ground bay leaves
1 teaspoon cayenne
2 tablespoons white pepper
1 teaspoon nutmeg
1 teaspoon allspice
1 tablespoon mace
1 tablespoon celery seed
1 tablespoon fine ground cloves

Mix all the ingredients together, and rub into your favorite grilling vegetables. Store remaining rub in an airtight container.

Smoke That Brisket Rub

1 cup brown sugar
1 minced green chili
1/2 cup chili powder
2 tablespoons cayenne
1 tablespoon freshly ground black pepper
1 tablespoon Accent
1 tablespoon minced garlic

Mix all the ingredients together, and rub into all sides of brisket. Allow to rest in the refrigerator for at least 12 hours before grilling or smoking.

Bag 'Em and Tag 'Em Wild Game Rub

1/4 cup sugar
2 tablespoons paprika
1 tablespoon onion powder
2 tablespoons seasoned salt
1 tablespoon garlic powder
1/2 tablespoon chili powder
1/2 tablespoon lemon pepper
1 tablespoon dried sage
1/2 teaspoon dried basil
1/2 teaspoon dried rosemary
1/2 teaspoon cayenne pepper

Mix all the ingredients together, and rub well into your favorite wild game meat. Allow the rub to work at least 30 minutes before grilling.

Savanna Brown Sugar Brisket Rub

¹/₂ cup brown sugar
¹/₂ cup smoked salt
¹/₂ cup paprika
¹/₂ cup chili powder
¹/₂ cup ground black pepper
¹/₄ cup Accent

Mix all the ingredients together, and pack firmly around the brisket. Place seasoned brisket wrapped in plastic in the cooler, and let stand for at least 12 hours before grilling or smoking.

Dry rubs will keep up to six months in a tightly closed container. If you're planning on storing a large batch of dry rub, use the most recently purchased dried herbs and spices. Remember, most will lose their flavor after the package or bottle has been open for six months.

Always allow a rub to work the meat for at least 15 minutes or more. If applying a rub to chicken, turkey, or pheasant with the skin on, remember to also place rub under the poultry skin.

I recommend lightly scoring the meat to help the rubs penetrate farther.

Always keep the rubbed food in the fridge until ready to grill.

COUSIN RICK'S TOP TEN SIGNS YOU'RE AT A BARBECUE THAT'S GONE BAD!

10. Everything on the grill has a long, thin tail.
9. To avoid burning, chicken breasts are covered in Coppertone.
8. The "cole slaw" is just mayonnaise and lawn trimmings.
7. The three-legged race is won by a three-legged kid.
6. Every couple of minutes the cook yells, "It's okay, just pull the dirt off."
5. The host tells you that the burgers are 20 percent beef and 80 percent critter.

4. The steaks have been sitting in marinade all night, and so has your Grandpa's ear!

3. You have to sign a legal waiver before you eat the potato salad.

2. The cook tosses a piece of hog for the dog to chew on, and he runs away yelping.

1. The guests all have grill marks on their foreheads.

WET RUBS

Grillin' Hick Rub

4 cups minced real bacon bits
2 cups minced parsley
2 cups tomato paste
$1/2$ cup cracked black pepper
$1/3$ cup paprika

Mix all the ingredients together, and rub into your favorite beef or pork. Store remaining rub in an airtight container. This is a thick pasty rub.

Louisiana Wet Rub

I cup minced yellow onion
I cup Creole mustard
2 tablespoons minced garlic
I tablespoon Louisiana hot sauce
$1/4$ cup Cajun seasoning
I tablespoon Accent

In a large bowl, mix all the ingredients together, and rub into ribs or roast. Let rub work the meat for at least 2 hours before grilling or smoking.

Wings of the Devil Rub

3/4 cup minced garlic
1 cup brown sugar
1/2 cup cider vinegar
1/4 cup minced red pepper
1/4 cup tomato paste
4 tablespoons hot pepper sauce
2 tablespoons garlic salt

In a large bowl, mix all the ingredients together, and rub into chicken or turkey wings at least 30 minutes before grilling.

"Honey Is That Your Mom?" Rub

1/2 cup virgin olive oil
8 minced garlic cloves
1 tablespoon minced parsley
1 teaspoon Accent
1 teaspoon cayenne

In a large bowl, mix the garlic, parsley, Accent, and cayenne together. Slowly add the virgin olive oil while stirring.

Rub the choice of meat on all sides, and let sit for at least 15 minutes before grilling.

Popeye Fish Paste

1/2 cup fresh spinach
1/3 cup olive oil
5 minced garlic cloves
1 teaspoon cayenne pepper
1 tablespoon fresh lemon juice
1 teaspoon lemon zest

In a large blender, combine all the ingredients, and mix until smooth. Rub both sides of your favorite fish, and let sit for 15 minutes before grilling. This recipe works wonders for fresh grilled salmon.

Kentucky Gobbler Rub

1/4 cup Worcestershire sauce
1/4 cup olive oil
5 teaspoons chopped rosemary
4 teaspoons chopped thyme
4 teaspoons minced white onions
4 teaspoons minced garlic
3 teaspoons garlic salt
2 teaspoons Kentucky bourbon

Combine all the ingredients together, and blend well. Coat all areas of a large turkey breast at least 30 minutes before grilling or smoking. This is a great rub to use when grilling wild turkey.

Horsing Around Rub

3/4 cup freshly grated horseradish root
1/2 cup minced garlic
1/4 cup quick salt
1/4 cup fresh ground black pepper
1/2 cup olive oil
2 tablespoons cumin
2 tablespoons Dijon mustard
2 tablespoons brown sugar
1 tablespoon Accent

In a large bowl, combine all the ingredients together, and blend well. This recipe works very well with prime rib and large cuts of steak or roast. Allow to rest into meat for at least 30 minutes before grilling.

Momma Mia Parmesan Pork Chop Paste

1/2 cup grated Parmesan cheese
1/2 cup olive oil
1/4 cup red vinegar
2 tablespoons oregano
2 tablespoons basil
1 tablespoon white pepper
5 minced garlic cloves

In a mixing bowl, combine all the ingredients together, and rub well into both sides of the chops 20 minutes before grilling.

Bird of Paradise Rub

1 chopped white onion
1 cup diced scallions
3 chopped hot peppers
1 tablespoon dried thyme
2 teaspoons garlic salt
1 teaspoon allspice
1 teaspoon white pepper
$^1/_2$ teaspoon cinnamon
$^1/_2$ teaspoon nutmeg

In a large blender, combine all the ingredients together, and blend until smooth. Rub all sides of your favorite poultry, let sit for 15 minutes, and grill.

Prime Rib Grillin' Paste

1 tablespoon minced garlic
2 tablespoons chopped fresh basil
3 tablespoons chopped fresh oregano
2 tablespoons chopped fresh parsley
2 tablespoons chopped fresh rosemary
5 tablespoons oil
2 tablespoons seasoning salt
1 teaspoon Accent
1 tablespoon white pepper

Combine all the ingredients in a food processor, and blend until smooth. Spread evenly over both sides of the prime rib roast, and grill on low heat.

Longhorn Hoedown Rub

5 tablespoons chili powder

5 teaspoons ground cumin

5 minced garlic cloves

3 tablespoons Worcestershire sauce

2 tablespoons garlic salt

3 tablespoons brown sugar

2 tablespoons black pepper

2 tablespoons allspice

5 tablespoons olive oil

In a large blender, blend all the ingredients together until even and smooth. Rub mixture into a large cut of beef, and let rub sit on meat for at least 2 hours before grilling on low.

Cheers! Rub

$1/2$ cup fresh thyme leaves

I cup green onions

3 tablespoons diced ginger

3 habanero peppers

$1/4$ cup peanut oil

6 chopped garlic cloves

2 teaspoons allspice

I teaspoon ground nutmeg

I tablespoon black pepper

I tablespoon ground coriander

I tablespoon ground cinnamon

2 teaspoons sea salt

$1/2$ cup fresh lime juice

In a large blender, blend all the ingredients together until even and smooth. Rub into your favorite meat, and let sit for an hour before grilling or smoking.

Osaka Wet Rub

1 chopped white onion

2 tablespoons peanut oil

2 teaspoons salt

1 teaspoon pumpkin pie spice

1 cup orange juice

1 teaspoon grated orange rind

1 pound cranberries

1 cup sugar

In a large blender or food processor, blend all the ingredients together until smooth. Rub into large cuts of fish or chicken, and let sit for at least 2 hours before grilling.

This is also a great rub for wild game and fowl.

Barbeque Commander Rub

By far one of my most used wet rubs.

3 tablespoons cumin powder
3 tablespoons curry powder
2 tablespoons paprika
2 tablespoons coriander seeds
3 tablespoons black peppercorns
1 tablespoon ground cinnamon
1 teaspoon salt
1/4 cup olive oil
2 minced garlic cloves
3 tablespoons oregano
1/2 cup minced cilantro
1 teaspoon Accent

In a large skillet, combine the cumin, curry powder, paprika, coriander seeds, peppercorns, cinnamon, and salt. Roast the ingredients until the spices begin to smoke, about 3 minutes on low heat. Transfer the roasted spices to a large mixing bowl and add the oil, garlic, oregano, cilantro, and Accent. Mix all the ingredients well, and place in the refrigerator for 2 days in an airtight baggie. When ready, rub this grilling paste into your favorite steaks or ribs and grill on low heat until done. This rub will last in the refrigerator in an airtight container up to 7 days.

COUSIN RICK'S BARBECUING "QUIZ WHIZ"

Think you're ready to entertain your backyard buddies with great grilling techniques and barbecuing know-how? Here's a cool little quiz to have fun with your guests and learn a few things for yourself. And you thought this was just another old cookbook!

1. When was grilling first discovered as a method of cooking?
   a. About 27,000 years ago when, according to paleontologists, man discovered fire—cooking food over fire naturally followed that discovery.

    b. In 1951, when George Stephen, of Weber Brothers, Metal Works, developed the first kettle-covered charcoal grill.

    c. In the late 1970s as consumers were looking for a more healthy cooking style.

2. What was Louis Armstrong referring to when he recorded "Struttin' with Some Barbecue" in 1927?

    a. Strutting around the New Orleans World's Fair barbecue festival.

    b. Walking with a sexy lady. According to old slang, the term *barbecue* means "sexually attractive young woman."

    c. A newly developed tangy red sauce called "barbecue."

3. What is one of the most popular grills used today?

    a. The charcoal grill.

    b. The gas grill.

    c. The electric grill.

4. What's the traditional grilled food at a Hawaiian luau?

    a. Grilled pineapple slices.

    b. Grilled poi.

    c. A whole hog, roasted to perfection by digging a pit in the earth filled with hardwood and slow-fire hot coals.

5. What's the leanest grilled cut of pork?

    a. Ribs.

    b. Tenderloin.

    c. Butt.

6. Where did the first outdoor barbecue feast take place?

    a. In Dallas, Texas, where Lyndon B. Johnson held an inaugural barbecue.

    b. In New Orleans at the first Mardi Gras.

    c. In Alexandria, Virginia, where George Washington spent three entire days feasting on pork in 1769.

7. What does the term *pig-pickin'* mean?

    a. In sixteenth-century Europe, pig-pickin' was a practice among the affluent population—a hog would be butchered, the desirable parts set aside for eating, and the remains tossed to the peasants for picking.

    b. A gathering of people, originally for political purposes, where a whole hog is barbecued and laid out for the guests to pull apart, hence the term "pulled pork."

    c. Someone who picks at food.

8. Where did the term *barbecue* originate?
    a. From Jacque de Barbecuet, the French-born inventor of the barbecue grill as we know it today.
    b. In colonial times, when the grilled dinners were often served at local bars.
    c. From the Mayans who cooked over a *barbacoa,* a lattice of thin green sticks suspended over an open fire.

9. What does grilling pork over direct heat mean?
    a. Placing the pork directly into the flames.
    b. Arranging the hot coals in an even bed on the fire grate of the grill and placing the pork above the heat source.
    c. Rotating the pork on a spit over open flames.

10. In recent times, which two presidents held large barbecue events during their campaigns?
    a. John F. Kennedy and Richard M. Nixon.
    b. Lyndon B. Johnson and Jimmy Carter.
    c. Ronald Reagan and Gerald Ford.
    d. George Bush and George Walker Bush.

Are you ready for the answers?
1. a.
2. b.
3. b.
4. c.
5. b.
6. c.
7. b.
8. c.
9. b.
10. c and d. The Bushes are well-known for their Texas barbecues. Ronald Reagan and Gerald Ford also held large barbecues during their campaigns.

CHAPTER TWO

BARBECUE SAUCES

This is the chapter you've been waiting for! Why, grillin' meat and barbecue sauce go together like Ted Nugent and a Les Paul guitar, like Dale Jr. and a fast set of wheels, like a lab on a duck, like stink on a skunk! Barbecue sauce is without a doubt the key factor in grilling and of course barbecuing.

I have put together my favorite barbecue sauces that cover everything from pork to fish.

Although some sauce recipes may appear to have very similar ingredients, it is how they are measured and developed that gives each sauce its own creative flavor.

The secrets of the following sauce recipes are well worth the few bucks you shucked out for this book!

Food Guru tip: My buddy Chef Peter Harman, the Food Guru, says food absorbs flavors as it cools down, so put an almost room temperature piece of meat in marinade and place it in the fridge. It will absorb the marinade like a sponge. For even more tips, visit www.foodguru.com, and tell Peter that Cousin Rick says howdy!

Try each sauce, and then develop your own flavor to satisfy your taste buds!

Mississippi Grillin' Sauce

1 gallon cider vinegar
$1/4$ cup salt
2 tablespoons red pepper
2 tablespoons red pepper flakes
$1/2$ cup molasses

Mix all the ingredients together, and let stand for about 4 hours before using on your favorite grilled meats.

Jeff May's BBQ Chicken Sauce

16-ounce can of stewed Mexican-style tomatoes
3 tablespoons brown sugar
2 tablespoons soy sauce
1 teaspoon dry mustard
$1/2$ teaspoon creamed horseradish
$1/2$ teaspoon Tabasco sauce

Combine all the ingredients in a small saucepan, bring to a boil, reduce the heat to a simmer, and cook for about 10 minutes.

Dr. Franks' Micucci Sauce

2 cups cider vinegar
$1/2$ cup beer
$1/2$ cup ketchup
1 teaspoon garlic salt
1 chopped white onion
2 tablespoons brown sugar
1 tablespoon Worcestershire sauce
$1/4$ teaspoon red pepper flakes

Mix all the ingredients together in a saucepan, and gently boil for about 20 minutes while stirring.

Vista Sauce

1 cup white vinegar
1 cup cider vinegar
1 tablespoon brown sugar
1 tablespoon crushed red pepper flakes
1 tablespoon Tabasco sauce
$1/4$ teaspoon white pepper
$1/4$ teaspoon garlic powder

Combine all the ingredients together in a large mixing bowl, let stand for 20 minutes, and use.

Montego Sauce

2 cups cider vinegar
1 tablespoon peppercorns
1 teaspoon celery seeds
1 teaspoon garlic salt
1 tablespoon hot pepper flakes
1 minced white onion
1 cup dark beer

Combine all the ingredients in a large saucepan. Bring to a boil, reduce heat, and simmer uncovered for about an hour. Strain to remove the peppercorns.

Better an Old Dog than a Dead Lion Sauce

1 gallon water
1 quart ketchup
1 quart white vinegar
12 ounces brown sugar
8 ounces garlic salt
4 ounces white pepper
4 ounces crushed red pepper flakes
1 teaspoon cayenne

Combine all the ingredients into a large pot, and boil, stirring occasionally. Simmer for about 30 minutes on low heat.

My Old Dogs Be Hurtin' Sauce

1 cup apple cider vinegar
1 teaspoon garlic salt
1 teaspoon celery salt
$1/2$ cup ketchup
$1/2$ teaspoon chili powder
$1/4$ teaspoon nutmeg
$1/2$ teaspoon brown sugar
1 cup water

Combine all the ingredients together, and stir. Bring to a boil in a saucepan, and simmer on low for about 5 minutes.

What's Up Homeboy Sauce

1 cup apple cider vinegar
2 tablespoons garlic salt
$1/2$ teaspoon red pepper flakes
1 tablespoon brown sugar

Combine all the ingredients together, and let stand for 6 hours.

224th War Sauce

2 cups cider vinegar
$1/2$ cup ketchup
I teaspoon salt
$1/2$ teaspoon ground red pepper
$1/4$ teaspoon red pepper flakes
I tablespoon sugar
$1/2$ cup beer

Combine all the ingredients in a saucepan, and bring to a boil; then simmer and stir until sugars are dissolved.

Cousin Rick's #44 Hot BBQ Sauce

$1/2$ cup ketchup
$1/4$ cup beer
$1/4$ cup chopped white onions
3 tablespoons red wine vinegar
2 tablespoons olive oil
2 teaspoons brown sugar
2 teaspoons Worcestershire sauce
2 teaspoons whole mustard seeds
I teaspoon paprika
$1/2$ teaspoon dried crushed oregano
$1/2$ teaspoon chili powder
$1/2$ teaspoon garlic salt
$1/4$ teaspoon ground cloves
I minced garlic clove
I bay leaf

In a large saucepan, combine all the ingredients together, and bring mixture to a boil. Reduce heat, and simmer for about 15 minutes, stirring often. Discard the bay leaf.

Honk if You're Horny
Lemon Mustard Sauce

$1/2$ cup mayonnaise
$1/2$ cup sour cream
3 tablespoons lemon juice
3 tablespoons Dijon mustard
$1/2$ teaspoon garlic salt
$1/2$ teaspoon white pepper

Combine all the ingredients together in a large bowl, and mix thoroughly. Serve chilled on your favorite grilled meat.

Old Man Burgess Soggy Bottom
BBQ Sauce

1 cup yellow mustard
$1/2$ cup white balsamic vinegar
$1/3$ cup brown sugar
2 tablespoons butter
2 tablespoons Worcestershire sauce
1 tablespoon lemon juice
1 tablespoon molasses
1 tablespoon cayenne pepper

In a saucepan, mix all the ingredients together, and simmer over low heat for about 35 minutes.

Table Rock Lake BBQ Sauce

1 cup dry red wine
1/4 cup red wine vinegar
1/4 cup olive oil
3 tablespoons Worcestershire sauce
2 tablespoons soy sauce
1 chopped white onion
1 tablespoon brown sugar
1 tablespoon grated orange zest
1 teaspoon ground ginger
4 chopped garlic cloves

Combine all the ingredients together in a large blender or food processor, and blend until the mixture is even and smooth. Transfer blended ingredients to a large saucepan, and bring the mixture to a boil. Reduce the heat and simmer uncovered for about 20 minutes, stirring often.

Rightly Ribs BBQ Sauce

1 can tomato sauce
1 chopped onion
6 ounces tomato paste
6 finely chopped scallions
1 tablespoon minced ginger
4 minced garlic cloves
1 teaspoon cayenne
1/2 teaspoon garlic salt

In a saucepan, combine all the ingredients together, and simmer over low heat for about 15 minutes. When finished cooking, place the ingredients into a blender, and blend until the mixture is smooth.

Tide's BBQ Basil Fish Sauce

4 tablespoons butter
I tablespoon olive oil
I teaspoon minced garlic
2 cups chopped tomatoes
I chopped red onion
$1/4$ cup fresh lemon juice
$1/2$ teaspoon garlic salt
$1/2$ teaspoon white pepper
$1/2$ teaspoon sugar
I teaspoon dried basil

In a large saucepan, heat all the ingredients, and simmer on low heat for about 20 minutes or until the tomatoes are very tender. Place the simmered ingredients into a food processor, and blend until the mixture is even and smooth. Serve on your favorite grilled fish.

Chopper's BBQ Sauce

3 cups chopped yellow onions
$1/4$ cup honey
I tablespoon chopped garlic
3 tablespoons lemon juice
I cup chopped sweet peppers
I tablespoon Accent
$1/2$ cup dried parsley
3 tablespoons Worcestershire sauce
I cup dry white wine
$1/2$ teaspoon dried mint
I tablespoon liquid smoke
2 cups ketchup
I tablespoon hot sauce

In a large saucepan, place all the ingredients together, and bring to a boil; cook, covered, on low heat for about $1^1/2$ hours. Stir this mixture often.

Denny Big Feet's BBQ Sauce

1 cup blackberry preserves
3 cups ketchup
$1/4$ cup brown sugar
$1/2$ teaspoon cayenne
$1/2$ teaspoon mustard powder
2 tablespoons red wine vinegar
1 teaspoon Accent

In a large mixing bowl, combine all the ingredients, and mix well. Let sauce stand for about an hour before using on your favorite grilled chicken or ribs.

Daily Gate City Grill Sauce

1 cup maple syrup
1 cup ketchup
1 cup minced onions
$1/4$ cup brown sugar
$1/4$ cup apple cider vinegar
$1/4$ cup lemon juice
$1/4$ cup dark beer
2 tablespoons olive oil
3 tablespoons Worcestershire sauce
2 tablespoons minced garlic
2 teaspoons grated lemon peel
1 teaspoon Accent
1 teaspoon Louisiana hot sauce

In a large saucepan, bring all the ingredients to a boil, and then simmer on low heat for about 25 minutes. Allow mixture to cool, and then blend in a food processor until even and smooth.

Hop Sing's BBQ Sauce

$1/4$ **cup soy sauce**
$2/3$ **cup white wine vinegar**
$1/2$ **cup pineapple juice**
$1/2$ **teaspoon ground ginger**

Combine all the ingredients in a large mixing bowl. Allow mixture to stand for about 45 minutes before using on your favorite chops and steaks.

Rocky Top Onion BBQ Sauce

4 tablespoons butter
6 cups minced onions
$1/2$ **cup vermouth**
3 tablespoons flour
2 cups chicken broth
$1/2$ **cup beer**
$1/2$ **teaspoon garlic salt**
$1/2$ **teaspoon white pepper**

Heat the butter in a large, deep skillet over medium heat, and sauté the onions, stirring often.

Add the remaining ingredients, and simmer on low heat for about 45 minutes, or until the BBQ sauce has thickened to your liking. This is a great BBQ sauce for grilling lamb.

Stockport Garlic Sauce

I lemon
I peeled and chopped orange
I peeled and chopped grapefruit
4 minced garlic cloves
$^1/_2$ cup dry white wine
I tablespoon olive oil
I teaspoon fresh chopped thyme
$^1/_2$ teaspoon garlic salt
$^1/_2$ teaspoon white pepper

Peel the lemon and chop the yellow zest until very fine. Peel the remaining white pith from the lemon and cut into cubes. Combine the lemon cubes with the orange and grapefruit, and set aside. Combine the remaining ingredients in a saucepan, and bring the mixture to a boil. Reduce the heat, and simmer for about 15 minutes. Stir in the lemon zest and the remaining fruit, and simmer on low heat for another minute.

Serve with your favorite grilled fish and chicken. This is also a great sauce for grilled cornish hens.

Braising Billy's BBQ Sauce

4 chopped garlic cloves
$1/4$ cup olive oil
1 teaspoon Accent
1 teaspoon cayenne
$1/2$ teaspoon dried oregano
1 tablespoon chopped basil leaves
2 cups pureed tomatoes
$1/4$ cup honey
$1/2$ cup red wine
$1/2$ cup dark beer
$1/4$ cup lime juice
$1/4$ cup chopped parsley

In a large saucepan, combine all the ingredients, and bring to a boil. Reduce the heat, and simmer for about 20 minutes on low heat. After the mixture has cooled, blend in a large blender until the sauce is even and smooth.

Rick's Maine Lobster BBQ Sauce

1 cup mayonnaise
$1/2$ cup ketchup
$1/2$ cup lemon juice
2 tablespoons Worcestershire sauce
2 tablespoons minced white onions
2 tablespoons sugar
$1/2$ teaspoon garlic salt
$1/2$ teaspoon white pepper

Mix all the ingredients together thoroughly, and allow it to rest for about an hour in the cooler before brushing on your favorite lobster tails.

Cousin Rick Black's Award-Winning Secret Pit BBQ Sauce

Of all the cookbooks I have written, this is the very first time this family secret pit barbecue sauce has been printed. I have never shared this recipe, other than with immediate family members, until now. Enjoy!

2 chopped white onions
1 chopped tomato
2 bay leaves
2 minced garlic cloves
4 tablespoons butter
1 tablespoon chili powder
1 cup ketchup
$^1/_2$ cup dark beer
1 shot Kentucky Sour Mash Bourbon
4 tablespoons cider vinegar
3 tablespoons light brown sugar
2 tablespoons prepared mustard
2 tablespoons virgin olive oil
1 teaspoon hot pepper sauce
1 teaspoon Accent
1 teaspoon white pepper
1 sliced orange
1 teaspoon peanut butter

In a large saucepan, cook the onion and garlic in butter until they are tender. Add the remaining ingredients except the orange slices and peanut butter. Bring the mixture to a boil, and remove from heat.

Let the mixture stand for 30 minutes while stirring often. Add the orange slices and peanut butter, and simmer on low heat for another 5 minutes, again stirring often. Serve this special barbecue sauce on all your favorite grillin' vittles!

Hannibal Park BBQ Sauce

2 cups Western-style dressing
2 cups apple butter
2 cups ketchup
I cup Worcestershire sauce
I teaspoon garlic salt
I teaspoon white pepper
I teaspoon Accent

In a large bowl, combine all the ingredients, and store in the cooler until ready to use on your favorite ribs or chops.

Oink Sauce

I cup butter
I cup bacon drippings
5 tablespoons lemon juice
2 tablespoons Worcestershire sauce
2 tablespoons garlic powder with parsley flakes
I teaspoon salt
2 teaspoons pepper
2 tablespoons chili powder
I cup beer
2 cups water

In a large pot, combine the butter, bacon drippings, lemon juice, and Worcestershire sauce. Cook over medium heat until the butter melts. Dissolve the chili powder, salt, pepper, and garlic powder with parsley in the beer, and add to butter mixture. Add the water, and bring to a boil. Simmer the sauce for 30 minutes on low heat, stirring often.

Schmitty's Ozark Melon BBQ Sauce

1 medium-sized seedless watermelon
10 ounces tomato paste
2 tablespoons garlic powder
1 tablespoon onion salt
2^1/$_2$ cups brown sugar
^{1}/$_2$ cup sherry
1 tablespoon orange juice
1 tablespoon liquid smoke
1 teaspoon Accent

In a large saucepan, cut the melon into 2-inch cubes, and cook uncovered until it becomes a thick sauce. Add the remaining ingredients, and simmer for about 1^1/$_2$ hours on low heat. Stir the sauce while simmering about every 10 minutes or so. Let sauce cool before using on your favorite grilled meats.

Tornado Alley BBQ Sauce

1 cup dark Karo syrup
1 cup dark coffee
^{1}/$_2$ cup ketchup
^{1}/$_2$ cup cider vinegar
^{1}/$_2$ cup Worcestershire sauce
3 tablespoons chili powder
1 tablespoon corn oil
1 tablespoon dry mustard
1 teaspoon garlic salt
1 teaspoon pepper sauce

In a large mixing bowl, combine all the ingredients, and stir until all is even and smooth.

Cover the bowl, and let rest in the cooler for about 4 hours before using on your favorite grilled foods.

Grillin' Like a Villain Sauce

1 tablespoon black pepper

1 teaspoon onion salt

1 teaspoon white pepper

1 tablespoon minced garlic

1 teaspoon cayenne pepper

$^1/_2$ pound minced bacon

2 cups minced white onions

1 cup pork stock

1 cup beer

2 cups chili sauce

1 cup honey

1 cup dry roasted chopped cashews

$^1/_4$ cup orange juice

1 tablespoon lime juice

1 tablespoon hot sauce

5 tablespoons butter

In a large saucepan, fry the bacon until dark and crisp. Stir in the onions, and cook until tender. Stir in the remaining ingredients, and bring to a boil. Reduce heat, and simmer mixture on low heat for about 30 minutes. Let the mixture cool, and then blend in a food processor until the sauce is even and smooth. This is a great sauce with ribs, steaks, chops, and chicken. Store leftover sauce in the cooler up to 7 days.

COUSIN BUBBA'S TIPS ON BBQ

These tips are from Cousin Bubba's BBQ cookbook.

The only problem is that Bubba couldn't find a publisher to print it.

Bubba strongly feels that this was unjust. You be the judge.

1. A clean grill is essential. You can spend a lot of time scrubbing your grill with a wire brush, or you can load up your guests on beer and alcohol and they won't even notice your filthy grill.

2. You can remove the base rock and racks and scrape out any debris from last season, or you can as already mentioned load up your guests on beer and alcohol and they won't even notice your filthy barbecue.

3. Before placing food on the barbecue for the first time, give the barbecue a good burn off for ten minutes, and then wipe with clean vegetable oil. This will burn onto the grill or griddle and reduce the likelihood of food sticking. You can also soak your food in vegetable oil, which will prevent your food from sticking when you flip it over. Or brush the hot grill with WD-40 before cooking.

4. Sprinkle the coals with herbs while you're cooking. This gives off a lovely aroma and keeps the flies away.

5. Keep all your barbecuing tools handy. Tongs, chopping boards, insulated gloves, basting brushes . . . and don't worry about making sure that they are thoroughly cleaned and dried before putting them away. This will give your next barbecue even more flavor.

6. Don't try to cook your food too soon. Leave your coals to heat up for at least three or four days first.

7. If you're a sissy, thoroughly cook your food for that burnt-to-a-crisp flavor.

8. For low-fat grilling, use herbs and salt instead of oil.

9. For low-salt grilling, use herbs and oil as a salt substitute.

10. For low-fat, low-salt, low-herb grilling, eat a stinking salad!

11. To avoid sending smoke signals to guests and neighbors, trim off excess fat and drain food that has been marinating. Unless of course you hate your neighbors—then place your barbecue grill so the wind will blow your smoke directly in their direction. Also be sure to add extra fat to thicken the smoke.

12. As much as possible, keep the cooler in the shade, or better yet, keep your cooler in your refrigerator.

13. Speaking of coolers, never toss out the burnt meat; that's why you have a mother-in-law.

CHAPTER THREE

GRILLIN' AND BARBECUING APPETIZERS

This chapter is plum full of my favorite "gettin' it started" recipes. Doin' a BBQ and not havin' appetizers is like huntin' tree rats with no bullets! So get yourself organized and have everything ready. Fire up the deluxe grill and let's cook up some appetizer vittles!

Who Choked Art?

$^1/_2$ **cup olive oil**
4 tablespoons chopped tarragon
$^1/_2$ **cup lemon juice**
$^1/_2$ **teaspoon garlic salt**
$^1/_2$ **teaspoon white pepper**
10 artichokes

In a large mixing bowl, add the olive oil, tarragon, lemon juice, garlic salt, and white pepper. Mix well with a wooden spoon.

Clean the artichokes of leaves and leaf tips. Cut them in half. Place the 20 artichoke halves in the olive oil marinade, and let set at room temperature for 2 hours.

Place the marinated artichokes in the center of the grill, and cook for about 30 minutes while brushing with the remainder of the marinade.

Charcoal Bread

6 cups self-rising flour
2 cups water
1 tablespoon sugar
Melted butter

In a large mixing bowl combine the flour, water, and sugar. Mix the ingredients well to make good stiff bread dough. Knead, and add more flour if needed. Form the dough 3 tablespoons at a time into dough balls. On a floured surface, roll out balls into hot-dog-sized shapes. Lightly oil skewers, and push them into the shaped rolls. Place the rolls on the grill, and cook for about 15 minutes, turning often, while brushing on melted butter. Serve hot.

Shroom'n Kabobs

I pound whole button mushrooms
¹/₂ pound bacon
10 ounces barbecue sauce
Bamboo skewers

Soak the bamboo skewers for about 25 minutes in warm water. Cut the bacon strips in half.

Wrap each mushroom with a bacon slice, and place on a bamboo skewer. Grill for about 15 minutes, while basting with the barbecue sauce.

BBQ Mushroom Steaks

8 whole portabella mushroom tops
¹/₂ cup olive oil
I teaspoon minced garlic
¹/₂ teaspoon white pepper
Mozzarella cheese

In a small bowl mix the olive oil, minced garlic, and white pepper together, and brush onto both sides of the mushroom tops. Grill both sides of the mushrooms on low heat, and top with mozzarella cheese. Serve when the cheese is melted and the mushrooms are hot.

Wayne's Sweet Kielbasa

10 ounces maple syrup
10 ounces Dijon mustard
1 pound kielbasa

Mix together the maple syrup and Dijon mustard. Cut the sausage into 1-inch chunks. Place the sausage chunks on a well-soaked skewer. Cover and rub the skewered meat with the sweet mustard sauce.

Grill for about 20 minutes, turning frequently, and serve hot.

Amy McCoy's Funions

4 Vidalia onions
4 tablespoons butter
4 chopped garlic cloves
4 slices American cheese
Salt and pepper to taste

Peel the onions, and cut each into quarters, trying to keep the onion together. Place one tablespoon of butter and one whole garlic clove into the middle of each onion. Wrap the onions twice with foil, and place in the center of grill. Cook for about 30 minutes. Top with cheese, and serve when the cheese is soft and melted.

"Man Those Critters Is Hot!" Chilies

8 small poblano chilies
2 tablespoons olive oil
$^1/_2$ teaspoon garlic salt
$^1/_4$ teaspoon pepper
8 ounces chopped pepper Jack cheese
1 cup hot salsa

Halve each pepper lengthwise, keeping the stem intact; remove the seeds and membranes.

Brush the peppers with olive oil and season well with the garlic salt and pepper. Stuff each pepper with cheese and salsa and place on the grill for about 12 minutes or until the peppers are tender and the cheese is melted. Serve with ice-cold beer.

Sweet Drums

8 ounces maple syrup
10 tablespoons chili sauce
1 cup minced onion
5 tablespoons cider vinegar
2 tablespoons Dijon mustard
2 tablespoons Worcestershire sauce
5 pounds drumsticks

Combine the maple syrup, chili sauce, vinegar, mustard, and Worcestershire sauce in a large dish. Marinate the chicken drumsticks for about 6 hours in the fridge. Grill until the drumsticks are thoroughly cooked, basting often.

Hartschuh's Bad Breath Bread

1 stick soft butter
3 minced garlic cloves
1 teaspoon white pepper
1 loaf Italian bread

Mix the butter, garlic, and pepper in a mixing bowl. Slice the bread and spread the butter on one side of all slices. Place the bread slices back into a loaf form, and wrap with foil. Place the bread on the grill, and cook until it is golden brown like toast. Great with steaks!

Sherry Shrimp

12 large shrimp prawns, shelled and deveined
$^1/_4$ cup soft butter
1 cup orange juice
3 tablespoons cooking sherry
1 teaspoon grated orange zest
1 teaspoon grated ginger root
$^1/_4$ minced green onions
12 bamboo skewers

Soak the bamboo skewers in warm water for about 30 minutes. Push the skewers through the shrimp from head to tail. Combine all the remaining ingredients together in a saucepan, and simmer for about 10 minutes on low heat.

Dip the skewered shrimp into the sauce, and grill on all sides for about 3 minutes per side, basting with remaining orange sauce.

Pablo's Peppers

1 pound seasoned pork sausage
30 jalapeño peppers
8 ounces soft cream cheese
2 pounds bacon

In a large skillet over medium heat, cook the sausage until browned. Drain, and set aside. Meanwhile, slice the peppers in half lengthwise, and remove the seeds and membrane. Fill one half of each pepper with cream cheese and the other half with cooked sausage. Put the pepper halves back together, and wrap with a slice of bacon. Use a toothpick to secure the pepper halves. Place the peppers on the grill, and cook for about 20 minutes, or until the peppers are toasted and the bacon is cooked.

Salmon Sticks

2 pounds skinless salmon filets
$1/2$ cup soy sauce
$1/2$ cup honey
2 tablespoons vinegar
1 tablespoon minced ginger root
2 minced garlic cloves
$1/4$ teaspoon white pepper
24 lemon quarters
24 bamboo skewers

Soak the bamboo skewers in warm water for about 30 minutes. Slice the salmon lengthwise into 24 strips. Thread each strip with a skewer. Place the skewered fish in a dish.

In a saucepan, stir in the soy sauce, honey, vinegar, ginger, garlic, and pepper. Simmer on low heat for about 10 minutes. Let sauce cool to room temp, and pour this sauce over the fish.

Marinate fish in the sauce for 15 minutes, and grill for 5 minutes per side, basting the fish with the remaining sauce.

Tasty Grilled Onion

I large sweet onion
2 tablespoons butter
I tablespoon minced garlic
Salt and pepper to taste

Peel the onion, and slice into 6 wedges, leaving the base intact. Pull the wedges apart, and add butter, garlic, salt and pepper. Wrap the onion in foil, and grill for about 35 minutes, or until the onion is tender and brown.

Iowa Grilled Shrimp

16 large shrimp, peeled and deveined
16 slices of thick-cut bacon
16 ounces ice-cold beer
16 large toothpicks

Soak the shrimp in beer for about 30 minutes. Wrap the bacon around the shrimp, and secure with toothpick. Grill the bacon and shrimp for about 5 minutes, turning once. The shrimp will be done when the bacon is fully cooked.

Dang Good Onions

4 large sweet onions, cut in wedges
16 thick slices of smoked bacon
4 tablespoons brown sugar
4 tablespoons balsamic vinegar
2 tablespoons molasses

Wrap the onion wedges with the thick smoked bacon, secure with toothpicks, and place in a dish. Combine the sugar, vinegar, and molasses; drizzle over the onion wedges. Cover the onion dish with foil, and chill for 2 hours.

Remove the onions from dish, reserving the sauce. Grill for about 25 minutes with the lid closed. Baste the onions often with the remaining sauce.

Patio Popcorn

3 tablespoons unpopped popcorn
2 tablespoons oil
1 teaspoon chili powder
1 teaspoon garlic salt
3 large disposable foil pans
Aluminum foil

Combine popcorn, oil, chili powder, and garlic salt in the disposable pan; mix well. Place the pan inside another pan to double its thickness. Place the last pan over top to cover and secure all with the foil. Grill for about 8 minutes or until the corn stops popping, shaking well.

Napoleon Grillin' Bread

$1/2$ **cup chopped basil**
$1/2$ **cup chopped white onions**
$1/2$ **cup chopped tomatoes**
I cup olive oil
I teaspoon onion powder
$1/4$ **teaspoon white pepper**
$1/2$ **teaspoon curry powder**
$1/2$ **teaspoon garlic salt**
$1/2$ **teaspoon red pepper flakes**
$1/2$ **teaspoon cumin**
$1/4$ **teaspoon cayenne pepper**
I cup shredded mozzarella cheese
3 pizza dough crusts, store bought or homemade

Combine the olive oil, onion powder, white pepper, curry powder, garlic salt, red pepper flakes, cumin, and cayenne pepper in a sauce pan, and simmer for about 10 minutes on low heat, stirring often. Let the sauce cool on the stove for 1 hour. Brush both sides of the pizza crust with sauce, and place on the grill.

Cook each side for about 3 minutes, flip crust, and apply more sauce.

Top cooked bread with cheese, onions, basil, and tomatoes. Serve hot.

Livin' Large Taters

8 red bliss potatoes
2 quarts water
2 tablespoons salt
4 tablespoons olive oil
6 tablespoons sour cream
I tablespoon chopped chervil leaves
2 ounces caviar

Place the potatoes in a large saucepan; add the water and salt. Bring to a boil, cover, and simmer for about 25 minutes or until the potatoes are tender. Drain, and let the potatoes cool until they are easy to touch with hands. Cut a flat spot on each end of the potatoes, and cut the potatoes in half between the flat spots. With a small spoon or melon baller, scoop out the inside of the potatoes. Coat the potatoes with olive oil, and lightly salt them. Place the potatoes on the grill, and cook for about 10 minutes, turning once. Remove and let cool.

Once cooled, spoon 1 teaspoon of sour cream into each potato half. Sprinkle with chervil and top with caviar. (If your guests are like mine, don't tell them caviar is fish eggs!)

Grilled Cheesy Shrooms

I pound fresh mushrooms, stems removed
10 ounces blue cheese
2 large onions, sliced into rings
$^1/_4$ cup olive oil
I tablespoon garlic salt with parsley

Fill the mushroom caps with crumbled blue cheese, and coat the outside of the mushrooms with olive oil. Place the onion slices and mushrooms on the grill cheese side up.

Grill until the cheese has melted and the mushrooms are good and tender. Top with grilled onions, and season with garlic salt.

Fourth of July Mushrooms

24 fresh mushrooms
$^1/_4$ cup chopped green onions
3 tablespoons butter, divided
2 tablespoons flour
$^1/_2$ teaspoon marjoram
I tablespoon garlic powder with parsley
$^1/_4$ cup white wine
$^1/_2$ cup chopped ham

Remove the stems from mushrooms; reserve the caps. Chop the stems, and in a saucepan melt 1 tablespoon butter with chopped stems.

Blend in the flour, marjoram, and garlic powder; add the wine, and cook on low heat until bubbly. Stir in the chopped ham and green onions, and simmer on low heat, stirring often for another 2 minutes.

Stuff the mushroom caps with the ham mixture, and place the stuffed mushrooms in a buttered foil wrap. Grill for about 20 minutes, or until the mushrooms are good and tender.

GRILLIN' AT BUBBA'S

Bubba is always braggin' that he is the best outdoor cook this side of Charcoalville. It was at the local watering hole that his wife Merdell announced the true secrets of Bubba's cookin'.

1. Merdell goes to the store.
2. Merdell fixes the salad, vegetables, and dessert.
3. Merdell prepares the meat for cooking, places it on a tray along with the necessary cooking utensils, and takes it to Bubba, who is lounging beside the grill, drinking a cold beer.
4. Bubba places the meat on the grill.
5. Merdell goes inside to set the table and check on the vegetables.
6. Merdell comes out to tell Bubba that the meat is burning.

7. Bubba takes the meat off the grill and hands it to Merdell.
8. Merdell prepares the plates and brings them to the table.
9. After eating, Merdell clears the table and does the dishes.
10. Bubba asks Merdell how she enjoyed her night off.

THE COUSIN RICK "BEER-B-Q" DIET

It seems that a lot of people are dieting recently, trying everything from an all-carbohydrate to an all-protein mix. However, your old cousin Rick has another suggestion, one that has worked through the ages: the "Beer-B-Q" diet. Personally, I have a "liquid dinner" every time I go to the watering hole on Saturday night!

- **Fact:** A lite beer has between 70 and 100 calories, is almost all water, and the part that ain't water is almost pure carbohydrates.
- **Fact:** The average diet recommends a daily caloric intake of 1,200 calories for women and 1,500 for men, if you want to lose the medically safe two to three pounds a week. On the "Beer-B-Q" diet, that equates to at least 12 beverages a day for women, and 15 for men. I find this to be a measurable goal.
- **Fact:** The alcohol in beer is a diuretic, which causes the water to flush out almost immediately, leading to a consistent workout regimen including deep knee bends (getting out of the chair), fast walking (very good for your heart), and squats (as the case may be).
- **Fact:** Drinking beer actually helps you sleep—even when you aren't necessarily tired. All that added rest is certain to help any sleep deprivation you may have experienced while counting calories on those fad diets. In addition, you may experience the occasional "How did I get here?" when you wake up, which always makes for lively conversation and possibly additional exercise if you have to sneak out and run home.
- **Fact:** The "Beer-B-Q" diet is good for your heart. After just one day of consuming your required 12 to 15 beers, you will certainly want to consume some aspirin, which is medically proven to help prevent heart attacks.

- **Fact:** On the "Beer-B-Q" diet, you can eat as much barbecue as you want. The only rule is that you cannot consume any grilled food until you have consumed at least half of the day's required beers. This way, the vittles will probably only stay in your body a short time.
- **Fact:** Beer drinking is often done in bars, where other forms of exercise are common. Dancing, for example, is a good way to build up a thirst, as is chasing young dance partners. If you really want to maximize your workout, try actually walking up to the bar versus using a waitress. To take this to the extreme, you could even get up and get someone else a beer, perhaps someone who is newer to the diet plan than yourself.
- **Fact:** Beer is cheaper than Jenny Craig.

Based on these facts, let's run through a given scenario for diet implementation.

Caution: This is a weekend diet plan and should be attempted during the work week by only the staunchest of dieters.

Monday through Thursday: Eat barbecue and basically be a slob.

Friday: Feeling "huge," swing by the liquor store and stock up. Go to favorite place of beer drinking and begin the consumption process (remember 12 for women, 15 for men).

Saturday: Wake up (as required) and lounge around all day, feeling slightly smaller after expunging any barbecue that you may have accidentally consumed.

Saturday (P.M.): Restart cycle, noticing that your appetite has still not returned. Perhaps only meet half of your appetite consumption goal due to an ongoing discussion with "the dog that 364 that bit you." This is a good thing, as only half consumption means less than 1,000 calories for the day, and you still don't feel hungry.

Sunday (A.M.): Wake up for mandatory sports day. This is a very convenient diet during football season, but it can be successfully implemented year-round. There is some major professional sport being played every day of the year except the day before and the day after the Major League All-Star game (that's a fact, look it up). Consumption on this day should be paced to cover the entire day—you don't want to peak too soon. Again, you notice a lack of appetite and are feeling thinner all the time. Don't forget the aspirin.

Monday: Return to work, feeling thinner, well rested, and surprisingly mellow. Mark your log book, and begin preparation for the upcoming weekend.

Cousin Rick
Your Fitness Guru

CHAPTER FOUR

GRILLIN' WITH PORK

Pork is by far one of the most popular grillin' meats eaten all over the earth. It has a juicy, tender texture with a tasty flavor that is complemented by a wide range of herbs and spices. Pork meat responds well to almost any type of marinade and sauce.

I have found that pork is also one of the simplest meats to cook on the grill. Lean, tender chops can be marinated or rubbed and then cooked over the grate or coals. Spareribs and baby back ribs can be baked and then grilled to achieve that irresistible grillin' flavor.

In this chapter I have put together my favorite barbecue and grilling pork recipes. Try each one, and make your backyard buddies happy campers! As a bonus, I even give you my instructions on how to roast a hog in the last recipe!

Cousin Rick's Spit Suckling

1 50–60 pound whole suckling pig
1 pound fresh ground black pepper
35 garlic cloves
Garlic powder
Salt
12 pounds white onions
6 pounds stuffing
4 cups oil
4 feet of chicken wire
2 cups chopped apples

Clean pig and dry it. Cut slits in the skin, and insert the garlic cloves. Coat the pig with oil. Prepare stuffing, and combine with chopped onions and apples. Pack the cavity with the stuffing, and stitch it closed. Wrap the pig in chicken wire lengthwise.

Coat with garlic powder, rosemary, salt, and pepper. Insert spit, and cook about 5 feet above a bed of coals 7 to 8 hours, turning often. Add seasoning often. The meat will be done when the internal temperature is 160 to 170 degrees. Unwrap wire, and serve with some good BBQ sauce.

Ti Grilled Pork Butts

5 pounds pork butt
$1/2$ cup liquid smoke
3 tablespoons rock salt
5 large bay leaves with rib removed

Score the pork on all sides, making $1/4$-inch-deep slits about 1 inch apart. Rub the salt into slits, and then rub all sides with the liquid smoke. Wrap the pork butts in leaves and then in aluminum foil, and seal tight. Let stand for 60 minutes in cooler. Place on preheated grill, and cook for 25 minutes per side. Then bake in a 400-degree oven for 4 hours, or until done. Let pork stand for 30 minutes after removing from oven before slicing and serving. Serve with homemade BBQ sauce.

Alisha's Apricot Spareribs

4 pounds pork spareribs
10 ounces undrained apricot halves
3 tablespoons ketchup
4 tablespoons brown sugar
2 tablespoons lemon juice
1 tablespoon Dijon mustard
1 teaspoon ginger
$1/2$ teaspoon garlic salt

In a covered grill, bank the hot coals. Place the ribs on the grill over a drip pan, cover, and cook for about 2 hours, turning occasionally. Meanwhile, mix the remaining ingredients together in a food processor. Brush the ribs generously with the sauce, basting and turning for about 35 more minutes.

Calie's Caribbean Pork Loins

6 thick-cut boneless pork loins
1 sliced red onion
1 cup lime juice
1 teaspoon cayenne
$1/4$ teaspoon pepper flakes

Combine the onion, lime juice, and peppers in a large dish and mix well. Marinate the loins in the fridge, covered, for at least 4 hours.

Remove the loins from the marinade, reserving the remaining marinade. Place pork on the grill for about 20 minutes, turning once. Heat the marinade in a small saucepan until boiling, and serve with the pork.

Green Bay Sausage Tailgate Dish

I pound fresh green beans, trimmed and halved
²/₃ pound quartered red potatoes
I large sliced yellow onion
I pound diced smoked pork sausage
I teaspoon garlic salt
I teaspoon white pepper
I teaspoon olive oil
I teaspoon butter
¹/₃ cup beer

On a large sheet of foil, place the green beans, potatoes, onion, and sausage chunks. Season with garlic salt and pepper, sprinkle with olive oil, and top with the butter. Tightly seal the foil around the mixture, leaving only a small opening. Pour the beer into the opening and seal.

Place the foil packet on the grill, and cook for about 30 minutes, turning twice, or until the sausage is browned and the veggies are tender. Cheer on number 4, and drink more beer!

Ode to Billy Joe's Pork Pinwheels

1 pound whole pork tenderloin
6 slices bacon
3/4 cup prepared mustard
1/2 cup honey
1/4 cup cider vinegar
3 tablespoons ketchup
1 tablespoon brown sugar
1 tablespoon Worcestershire sauce
1 teaspoon hot sauce
1 cup minced pecans
1 teaspoon salt
1/2 teaspoon pepper
1/2 teaspoon garlic powder
Metal skewers

Cut the tenderloin lengthwise into 1/4-inch slices. Separate slices; place on a cutting board, and place a slice of bacon on each pork slice. Starting at one end, roll up into a spiral, and secure with toothpicks.

Combine mustard, honey, vinegar, ketchup, brown sugar, Worcestershire sauce, and hot sauce in a mixing bowl. Reserve 1 cup of the sauce until ready to serve. Brush the remaining sauce over pork rolls. Combine pecans, salt, pepper, and garlic powder in another bowl. Cut each pork roll in half to form 2 pinwheels for a total of 12, and secure ends with the skewers.

Coat each pork pinwheel with the pecan mixture. Grill pinwheels on high for about 8 minutes on each side, or until the pork is fully cooked. Drizzle the reserved sauce over cooked pinwheels, and serve.

Villain Brats

1 pound bratwurst
2 cans beer
1 chopped white onion
$^1/_2$ pound butter

Put the brats, beer, onion, and butter in a pan, and simmer on the stove for 1 hour. Drain the brats, and brown on the grill.

Stillwater Spareribs

2 pounds pork ribs, cut crosswise
4 crushed garlic cloves
2 tablespoons peanut oil
2 tablespoons fish sauce
3 tablespoons hoisin sauce

Combine the hoisin sauce, fish sauce, peanut oil, and garlic in a bowl and mix well. Rub the ribs with the sauce to coat well. Cover marinated ribs in the refrigerator for 3 hours. Grill over a medium fire, turning once until the ribs are slightly charred and fully cooked. Serve with remaining sauce.

Biloxi BBQ Pork

2 pounds boneless pork loin roast
²/₃ cup **BBQ** sauce (homemade, you can do it now)
¹/₃ cup orange marmalade
1 teaspoon hot pepper sauce
¹/₂ teaspoon grated horseradish
1 teaspoon garlic salt
¹/₂ teaspoon white pepper

Season the pork loin with garlic salt and white pepper; place on the grill. Stir the remaining ingredients together, and baste the loins every 5 minutes with sauce. Cook the meat until the meat thermometer reads 160 degrees. Let the pork rest for 10 minutes before slicing to serve.

Captain Morgan Chops

6 boneless pork chops
4 tablespoons Captain Morgan rum
¹/₂ teaspoon ginger
2 tablespoons lime juice
2 tablespoons brown sugar
¹/₂ teaspoon garlic salt
¹/₂ teaspoon white pepper
1 minced garlic clove
³/₄ cup orange juice
1 cup chicken stock

Combine all the ingredients together, and marinate in the refrigerator for 24 hours. Remove the chops, and discard any leftover marinade. Grill the chops for about 12 minutes, turning once to brown both sides of the chops.

Smoked Pulled Pork

5 pounds pork butt
I quart apple cider vinegar
2 chopped chipotle peppers
5 minced garlic cloves
2 tablespoons salt
I tablespoon pepper

Mix all the ingredients together but the meat. Place the marinade in the refrigerator for 12 hours. Season the pork with a good dose of salt and pepper to taste. Smoke over hickory at 250 degrees for about 10 hours.

Let the smoked pork cool for 25 minutes, and pull the meat apart with a large fork. Chop the meat, and pour marinade over it. Mix the meat and marinade together, and serve.

Jammin' in the Sand Party Chops

4 center-cut pork chops
10 ounces soy sauce
I teaspoon Accent
I teaspoon pepper

Combine the soy sauce, Accent, and pepper together in a small bowl. Place the pork chops in a nonreactive dish, and pour the sauce over them. Marinate the pork chops in the refrigerator for 8 hours.

Grill the chops about 8 inches from the coals for about an hour, basting with sauce every 10 minutes.

Montrose-Style BBQ Smoker Ribs

3 pounds country-style ribs
2 cups BBQ sauce

Using a smoker-type cooker with lid, arrange charcoal with coals on only half the cooking area. Pour ¼ inch water into a 2-inch-deep baking pan. Stir in 3 tablespoons of BBQ sauce. Arrange the ribs in the pan, and parboil in preheated 300-degree oven for 40 minutes, turning twice.

Remove the ribs from the pan, and place them on a well-greased grill directly over the coals. Grill until brown on first side. Turn and brush BBQ sauce on cooked side. Grill until brown on the second side. After browning, move the ribs to area not directly over coals. Coat the second side with BBQ sauce, cover, and continue cooking for about 20 more minutes.

Ten-Gallon Hat Loins

2 whole pork tenderloins
6 tablespoons chili powder
2 teaspoons oregano
³/₄ teaspoon ground cumin
¹/₂ teaspoon Accent
2 crushed garlic cloves

Mix together chili powder, oregano, cumin, Accent, and garlic. Rub all surfaces of the tenderloins with sauce. Cover, and refrigerate for 24 hours.

Grill over hot coals, turning occasionally, for about 20 minutes. The pork is done when the meat thermometer reads 160 degrees. Slice and serve.

Cuddles' Favorite Baby Backs

5-pound rack baby back ribs, cut into 3-rib sections
1 tablespoon cumin
2 cups homemade BBQ sauce
1/2 cup chopped cilantro
4 tablespoons minced red onion
5 tablespoons Kentucky sour mash
4 teaspoons chili powder

Get your grill ready. Sprinkle the ribs with salt, pepper, and 1 teaspoon cumin. Place the ribs, meaty side up, on grill. Cover, and grill for about 15 minutes.

Meanwhile, mix the BBQ sauce, cilantro, onion, sour mash, chili powder, and remaining cumin in a saucepan on the side of the grill to keep sauce warm. Turn the ribs meaty side down. Cover, and grill another 10 minutes or until cooked through. Turn the ribs over again; brush meaty side generously with BBQ sauce. Cover, and grill ribs until the sauce gets thick on the meat. Serve with remaining BBQ sauce.

Manitou Springs Grilled Soda Loin

1/2 cup soy sauce
1 cup brown sugar
1 tablespoon Accent
1 cup plum jam
1 can black cherry soda
1 large pork tenderloin

Combine soy sauce, brown sugar, Accent, and jam in a saucepan over low heat; cook until well combined. Set aside 1/2 cup of mixture to use as a baste. Place the remaining sauce in a plastic seal bag with the soda and loin. Marinate in the refrigerator for 8 hours. Place the loin on the grill, and cook for about 25 minutes, until outside of meat is caramelized, basting with the reserved sauce. Let rest for 10 minutes, and then slice.

Sweet Momma Chops

4 center-cut pork chops
Juice of 4 lemons
1 teaspoon lemon pepper
2 tablespoons honey
$^1/_4$ teaspoon Accent

Marinate the chops in lemon juice for 3 hours. While the chops are marinating, sprinkle each chop on both sides with the lemon pepper. Place on the grill, and cook for 15 minutes on each side. Five minutes before each side is done, spread with honey. Before removing from grill, sprinkle one side lightly with Accent seasoning.

Amana Colonies Cookout

16 bratwurst
4 quarts beer
16 hoagie buns
1 quart sauerkraut
Dijon mustard
Cloves

Simmer bratwurst and cloves about 40 minutes in beer, and then grill to a light brown over charcoal. Serve in bun, topped with sauerkraut and mustard.

Fort Bragg Ham-on-a-Spit

 1 very large precooked ham
 2 cups apricot nectar
 2 tablespoons cornstarch
 2 tablespoons ice-cold water
 1/2 cup red wine vinegar
 1/2 cup brown sugar
 1 tablespoon yellow mustard
 1 teaspoon Accent
 1 tablespoon Louisiana hot sauce
 3 tablespoons chili sauce
 1 tablespoon garlic salt
 1 cup apricot jam
 Cloves

Place the ham on a spit over medium coals, and cook for 80 minutes, basting often with 1 cup of apricot nectar. Make the sauce by combining cornstarch and water and mixing until it becomes a smooth paste. Then add remaining ingredients. Bring to a boil, reduce heat, and simmer for 8 minutes, stirring constantly.

Remove the ham from spit, and score the surface in a diamond pattern. Brush the entire surface with sauce, embed the ham with cloves, and return it to the spit for another 60 minutes. Baste the ham every 5 minutes with sauce. Serve the remaining sauce with cooked ham.

Sunshine Basil Grilled Chops

 6 pork loin chops
 3 crushed garlic cloves
 6 tablespoons olive oil
 3/4 cup diced basil
 12 ounces frozen lemonade, thawed
 1 teaspoon garlic salt

Mix the last 5 ingredients, and reserve 1/2 cup of the marinade to brush on chops while grilling. Pour the remaining marinade over chops, and refrigerate them for 4 hours, turning twice. Grill the chops for about 25 minutes, turning once and basting them.

Rock Country-Style Spareribs

8 pounds country-style ribs, trimmed and cut into serving-sized pieces
2 cans beer
1 cup dark corn syrup
1 cup minced white onion
1 1/2 cups mustard
1/2 cup vegetable oil
2 tablespoons chili powder
4 minced garlic cloves

Place the ribs in a very large, shallow baking dish. In a large bowl, stir together the beer, corn syrup, onion, mustard, vegetable oil, chili powder, and garlic. Pour over the ribs, cover, and refrigerate for 12 hours.

Remove the ribs from the marinade. Grill 8 inches from the coals for about 50 minutes, or until the ribs are cooked and tender, turning and basting every 5 minutes.

Uncle Marvin's Grilled Salsa Loin

1 large bowl of salsa
1 large pork tenderloin
1/2 teaspoon thyme
1 teaspoon oregano
1/4 cup soy sauce
1/3 cup lime juice

Combine the lime juice, soy sauce, oregano, and thyme in a large seal-top plastic bag. Add loin, turning to coat all sides. Seal, and refrigerate for 12 hours. Remove the loin from the marinade. Grill, covered, 6 inches from coals for about 40 minutes, or until fully cooked, turning and basting every 5 minutes. Slice the cooked tenderloin and top with salsa.

Scobeyville BBQ Ham Steaks

$^1/_2$ cup orange marmalade
$^1/_4$ cup prepared mustard
1 tablespoon Worcestershire sauce
3 tablespoons Five Star Whiskey
$^1/_4$ cup water
6 (1-inch-thick) ham steaks, fully cooked

Combine the first five ingredients and mix well; pour into a large baking dish. Add the ham steaks, turning to coat; marinate in the refrigerator for 2 hours. Remove the steaks from the marinade, reserving marinade for basting. Place the ham steaks 5 inches from the coals; grill for about 45 minutes, turning frequently and basting with marinade.

Bag 'Em and Tag 'Em Chops

4 Iowa chops
$^1/_4$ cup butter, softened
1 tablespoon molasses
1 teaspoon lemon juice
1 teaspoon garlic salt
5 tablespoons coarsely ground black pepper

Stir together butter, molasses, and lemon juice with a fork. Cover and refrigerate. Rub chops on all sides evenly with black pepper. Grill chops over medium hot coals for 15 minutes, turning twice. Top each chop with sauce.

Key Largo BBQ Pork

3 pounds boneless pork loin
I can dark beer
$^1/_2$ cup dark corn syrup
$^1/_2$ cup minced onion
$^1/_3$ cup prepared mustard
$^1/_4$ cup vegetable oil
2 tablespoons chili powder
3 minced garlic cloves

Place the pork loin in a large, shallow pan. In a mixing bowl, stir together the remaining ingredients; pour over loin. Cover, and refrigerate for 6 hours, turning every 30 minutes. Remove the loin from marinade. Place over drip pan on grill. Grill covered, with banked charcoal. Baste every 10 minutes with marinade. Cook meat for about 2 hours, and serve while hot.

Orleans-Style BBQ Ribs

3 pounds baby back ribs
I cup homemade BBQ sauce
I teaspoon hot pepper sauce
$^1/_2$ teaspoon red pepper flakes
$^1/_2$ teaspoon onion powder
$^1/_2$ teaspoon garlic powder
$^1/_2$ teaspoon celery seed
$^1/_2$ teaspoon thyme

Parboil the ribs for about 45 minutes. Combine the remaining ingredients together in a saucepan; mix well. Bring sauce to a boil; reduce the heat, and simmer for 5 minutes, stirring often. Place the ribs bone side down, and grill uncovered for 40 minutes, turning every 10 minutes. Brush the ribs with BBQ sauce, and continue grilling for 20 minutes, turning and brushing with BBQ sauce after 10 minutes.

Ribs of a Drunken Sailor

5 pounds spareribs
I cup brown sugar
$^1/_2$ cup chili sauce
$^1/_2$ cup ketchup
$^1/_2$ cup rum
$^1/_2$ cup soy sauce
2 tablespoons Worcestershire sauce
I teaspoon dry mustard
3 minced garlic cloves
$^1/_2$ teaspoon pepper
$^1/_2$ teaspoon garlic salt

Cut the ribs into serving-sized pieces. Line a roasting pan with a double thickness of foil. Place the ribs in roasting pan, and seal them with foil. Bake for 60 minutes at 350 degrees. Unwrap ribs, and pour off drippings. Combine the remaining ingredients to make marinade, and pour half of the marinade over ribs. Continue baking for 70 minutes. Lay the ribs on the grill 6 inches from coals. Grill for 20 minutes, basting ribs with the remaining marinade every 5 minutes.

Central Lee Class of '80 Smoked Loin

I very large pork loin, rolled and tied
I teaspoon garlic salt
$^1/_2$ teaspoon black pepper
I teaspoon ginger
2 tablespoons vegetable oil
2 tablespoons apple cider vinegar
2 tablespoons chili sauce
$^1/_2$ cup packed brown sugar
I large can peaches, undrained

In a food processor, combine the garlic salt, pepper, ginger, oil, vinegar, chili sauce, brown sugar, and undrained peaches. Blend until very smooth.

Place the pork loin in a glass dish. Pour half of the sauce over loin; refrigerate, covered, for 8 hours. Refrigerate the remaining sauce.

Get the grill ready by arranging a drip pan surrounded by hot coals. Add hickory chips, dampened with water, to coals. Place the roast on grill over drip pan. Baste every 5 minutes with sauce until the center of the roast reaches 165 degrees. Let the roast stand for 20 minutes before slicing. Simmer the remaining sauce for 5 minutes, and top roast slices with warm sauce.

The Blacks' Family Reunion Grilled Ham

5-pound fresh boneless ham
$^3/_4$ cup chili sauce
$^1/_2$ cup wine vinegar
3 tablespoons lemon juice
I teaspoon dry mustard
I minced garlic clove
I teaspoon Accent

Place the ham on grill rotisserie, making sure the drip pan is in place. Grill the ham over low coals for 2 hours, or until the meat thermometer reads 160 degrees.

In a bowl, combine the chili sauce, vinegar, lemon juice, mustard, garlic, and Accent; mix well. Brush the ham every 10 minutes with the sauce during the last 60 minutes of grilling. Let the ham rest for 15 minutes before carving.

Uncle Joe's "Boy You Got to Be Plum Crazy" Ham Steak

I large fully cooked ham steak
$^1/_4$ cup plum preserves
I tablespoon prepared mustard
I teaspoon lemon juice
$^1/_2$ teaspoon Accent
$^1/_8$ teaspoon cinnamon

In a saucepan, combine the plum preserves, mustard, lemon juice, Accent, and cinnamon. Cook and stir for 5 minutes on low heat. Keep sauce warm. Grill the ham steak over medium coals for about 10 minutes. Turn the streak, and grill for 10 more minutes. Brush the steak on both sides with sauce during the last 5 minutes of grilling.

Schmitty's BBQ Pork Steaks

4 large pork steaks
2 tablespoons flour
1 teaspoon garlic salt
$^1/_2$ teaspoon white pepper
$^1/_4$ cup minced red pepper
1 tablespoon water
$^1/_8$ teaspoon cayenne
1 teaspoon caraway seeds

Trim all but a small amount of fat from the sides of the steak. Combine the flour, garlic salt, white pepper, red pepper, and water to make a smooth paste. Dip the steaks in the paste, place them on the grill, and cook for 1 minute per side to set the coating. Then grill for another 15 minutes, turning every 5 minutes. Brush with the remaining coating just before taking steaks from the grill. Top the steaks with the cayenne pepper and caraway seeds.

Pappy's Peppered Grilled Pork Chops

4 large pork chops
1 tablespoon honey
2 tablespoons brown sugar
1 tablespoon vegetable oil
2 tablespoons soy sauce
$^1/_4$ teaspoon fresh ground pepper
Juice and zest of half an orange
$^1/_4$ teaspoon garlic salt

Place the honey, brown sugar, vegetable oil, soy sauce, pepper, orange juice, orange zest, and garlic salt in a bowl, and mix well with a fork until smooth.

Cook the chops on the grill for 20 minutes, turning every 5 minutes and brushing with the sauce each time.

Donnellson Fairgrounds Beer-N-Brats

8 fresh bratwurst
2 teaspoons vegetable oil
1 tablespoon flour
$^1/_2$ teaspoon dried marjoram
$^1/_8$ teaspoon caraway seeds
1 teaspoon minced garlic
1 cup dark beer

Grill the brats for about 20 minutes, or until the centers are no longer pink, turning every 5 minutes.

In a saucepan, heat the oil and flour over low heat, stirring often, until the sauce is light brown in color. Add the marjoram, caraway seeds, and garlic. Slowly stir in the beer, and bring sauce to a slow boil; reduce the heat and simmer, stirring frequently, until the sauce thickens. Place the brats in the hot sauce, simmer for 3 minutes, and serve the brats with the beer sauce.

Cousin Rick's Hog Roast Recipe

Feeds about a hundred mouth-watering Q-critters.

Hog roaster (with rotisserie)
1 100-pound hog (call your butcher at least 2 weeks in advance)
1 quart lighter fluid
100 pounds charcoal
Knives, tongs, and serving forks
Putty knife
Serving trays or meat warmers
Light-gauge steel wire
12 roasting chickens
12 large yellow onions, peeled and quartered
12 garlic cloves
25 pounds apple sweet wood chips
Chicken wire
Cousin Rick's Hog Rub recipe

Rub all sides of hog with Cousin Rick's Hog Rub 12 hours before cooking. Place about 80 pounds of charcoal into the hog roaster, spreading evenly along the bottom. Pour 1 quart of lighter fluid over the coals in the roaster. Light the coals, and let them burn down until gray edges form.

Sprinkle the coals with apple chips that have been soaked for at least 8 hours. Bring the roaster to 400 degrees.

Prepare the hog by stuffing it with the chickens, garlic cloves, and onions. Sew the stomach opening with steel wire, and insert rotisserie bar. (Get a helper for this.)

Wrap the hog in 1-inch chicken wire, and place in the roaster. Cook the hog for about 10 to 12 hours, turning every hour with the rotisserie baste.

HOW TO TALK LIKE THE BBQ PROS!

Baste: To brush sauce on food while working to add moisture and flavor.

Brochette: Comes from the French, food cooked on a skewer, kebab.

Ceramic briquettes: Radiant materials compacted into brick shapes.

Charcoal briquettes: Compacted ground charcoal and coal dust, mixed with starch, to be used in charcoal grills as fuel.

Charcoal grate: The rack that holds the charcoal in place.

Charcoal grill: A grill that uses charcoal briquettes as fuel.

Chimney starter: A cylinder that holds hot coals for starting a fire.

Direct grilling: A method of quickly cooking food by placing it on a grill rack directly over the heat source.

Drip pan: A pan placed under food to catch the drippings when grilling.

Dry smoking: A method of cooking food by placing it on the grill rack indirectly over the heat source with the lid down and vents adjusted to give smoke.

Dumb attack: To burn your food.

Firebox: The bottom of the grill that holds the fire.

Flareups: Flames that are caused by fat dripping onto the coals.

Gas grill: A grill that is fueled by liquid propane.

Glaze: To form a glossy coating during cooking for flavor.

Grill basket: A wire basket that holds foods for grilling.

Grill rack: The grill grate or grid.

Indirect grilling: A method of grilling slowly, using one side of the heat source.

Kebabs: Chunks of meat and vegetables threaded on a skewer and then grilled.

Kettle grill: A round charcoal grill with a heavy cover.

Lava rock: Volcanic lava that is used as an alternative to ceramic briquettes in gas grills.

Lump charcoal: Carbon residue of wood that has been charred.

Marinate: To steep food in a liquid mixture before it is grilled. Adds flavor and tenderizes meat.

Medium doneness: The center of the meat is slightly pink to red in color.

Medium-rare doneness: The center of the meat is bright red.

Medium-well doneness: The center of the meat has little or no red.

Rotisserie: The spit or long metal skewer that suspends and rotates the food over the grill's heat source.

Rub: A blend of seasonings rubbed onto the food surface before grilling.

Skewer: A long, narrow metal or wooden stick inserted through chunks of meat and vegetables for grilling.

Smoker box: A small perforated metal container placed on a gas grill's lava rocks, or the grill rack of a charcoal grill, to hold wood chips and provide smoke.

Vents: Holes in a grill cover or smoker box. When open, air circulates, increasing the heat of the grill.

Wood chips: Natural wood added to a fire to impart a smoky flavor.

CHAPTER FIVE

GRILLIN' WITH BEEF

If you're a rootin', tootin', and straight shootin' beef grillin' fool, this chapter is the one you've been itchin' to get your paws on! From grillin' brisket to ribs, we cover it all right here in this chapter.

T-Bones Flair

4 thick T-bones, well trimmed
2 teaspoons salt
2 teaspoons oregano
2 teaspoons sweet paprika
2 teaspoons thyme
I teaspoon garlic powder
I teaspoon onion powder
I teaspoon Accent
I teaspoon black pepper
I teaspoon white pepper
$^1/_2$ teaspoon crushed red pepper

Combine the salt, oregano, paprika, thyme, garlic powder, onion powder, Accent, and peppers in a small bowl, and mix well. Press the seasonings evenly onto both sides of the steaks. Grill the steaks for about 15 minutes, turning once. Let the steaks stand for 5 minutes before serving.

Festus BBQ Roast

5-pound boneless rump roast
3 sliced garlic cloves
I teaspoon paprika
I teaspoon Accent
I teaspoon white pepper
$^1/_4$ teaspoon rosemary
$^1/_4$ teaspoon thyme
$^1/_4$ teaspoon curry

Cut slits on all sides of the roast, and insert the garlic slices. In a small bowl, mix the paprika, Accent, white pepper, rosemary, thyme, and curry. Rub the mixture over the roast. Place the roast on a prepared rotisserie, and cook for about 4 hours, or until the center of the roast is 150 degrees. Let the roast rest for 30 minutes before slicing.

Santana Grilled Beef Heart

1 pound beef hearts, trimmed of fat and silverskin
6 dried pulla chilies
2 tablespoons annatto seeds
1 peeled garlic clove
1 teaspoon cumin
$1/2$ cup red wine vinegar
1 chopped jalapeño pepper
1 teaspoon Accent
$1/2$ cup olive oil
2 teaspoons salt

In a saucepan, place the chilies in enough water to cover, and bring to a boil. Remove the chilies, and let stand 30 minutes to soften. Drain and discard the water. In a blender combine the chilies, annatto seeds, garlic, cumin, red wine vinegar, jalapeño, and Accent. Blend until the mixture is thick and smooth. Add the olive oil and salt, and blend for another 2 minutes. Cut the beef hearts into 1/2-inch strips. Place in a bowl, and toss with chili sauce to coat evenly. Cover, and marinate in the refrigerator for 8 hours. Thread the heart strips on a skewer, and grill until seared on all sides.

Cripple Creek Liver

2 pounds beef liver
1 cup lemon juice
1 teaspoon Accent
1 teaspoon cumin
$1/2$ teaspoon garlic salt
$1/2$ teaspoon garlic powder
$1/4$ teaspoon white pepper
1 large sliced tomato
1 sliced red bell pepper
1 large sliced white onion

Marinate the liver in lemon juice, Accent, cumin, garlic salt, garlic powder, and white pepper for 1 hour. Place foil on grill rack, and cook the livers until brown on both sides. Place the tomatoes, bell peppers, and onions on top of cooked livers, and cover with foil. Cook for about 10 more minutes, or until the veggies are tender. Serve hot.

Lonesome Dove Brisket

1 whole beef brisket

3 cups ketchup

$^3/_4$ cup packed brown sugar

2 cups chili sauce

2 cups wine vinegar

2 cups water

1 can beer

$^1/_4$ cup lemon juice

$^1/_2$ cup prepared mustard

1 tablespoon celery seed

5 tablespoons Worcestershire sauce

1 tablespoon soy sauce

2 minced garlic cloves

1 teaspoon hot pepper sauce

1 teaspoon ground black pepper

Combine all the ingredients except the brisket together in a large dish. Marinate the brisket in the sauce for 12 hours in the refrigerator, turning every 4 hours. Place the whole brisket on a hot grill to sear and brown the fat. Remove the brisket from the grill, and place in a large foil pan. Cover the pan tightly with foil, close the grill hood, and cook for about 4 hours, or until the meat is tender. Baste the meat with the sauce every 30 minutes on all sides.

Rodeo Steaks

2 large strip steaks
1 teaspoon garlic powder
1 teaspoon onion powder
1 teaspoon black pepper
1 teaspoon white pepper
1 teaspoon ground red pepper
³/4 cup steak sauce (homemade)
¹/4 cup melted butter

Combine all the dry spices together, and rub both sides of the steaks. In a small mixing bowl, combine the steak sauce and melted butter. Grill the seasoned steaks for 15 minutes, turning and brushing every 5 minutes with the butter sauce. Serve the steaks with remaining sauce.

BBQ Hick Burgers

2 pounds ground burger
¹/2 cup salsa
1 package dry onion soup mix
¹/2 teaspoon garlic powder
¹/2 teaspoon Accent

Mix all the ingredients together, and form ¹/2-inch-thick patties. Grill for about 12 minutes, turning twice. Serve on bun with lettuce, tomato, avocado, and additional salsa.

Ranch Hand Roast

2 teaspoons minced garlic cloves
1 teaspoon oregano
4 tablespoons wine vinegar
$1/2$ cup ground black pepper
16 ounces ranch-style dressing
5-pound beef roast

Place the roast in a zip-top plastic bag. Mix the remaining ingredients together, and pour over roast. Seal the bag, and carefully shake it to coat the roast. Refrigerate the roast for 8 hours, turning the bag every 2 hours. When the coals are ready, push them to the sides of the grill, leaving the center open. Place the roast in the center of the grill and cook for about 2 hours, or until the roast is done to your liking. Turn the roast every 20 minutes while cooking, basting with sauce.

Lancaster Grilled Sirloins

2 large sirloins
2 tablespoons vinegar
1 teaspoon Accent
$1/2$ teaspoon Tabasco sauce
1 minced white onion
1 cup soy sauce
3 tablespoons ginger
3 pressed garlic cloves

Combine all the ingredients, and marinate in a zip-top plastic bag for 8 hours in the cooler. Grill the steaks quickly over charcoal, basting every 10 minutes until desired taste and texture are reached.

Anderson's Backyard Burgers

$^1/_2$ cup lemon juice
$^1/_2$ cup melted butter
1 tablespoon Worcestershire sauce
1 teaspoon garlic salt
1 tablespoon dry mustard
8 large hamburger patties

Combine the first 5 ingredients together, and marinate the hamburger patties for 4 hours before grilling.

Swampland Grill Jerky

$^1/_2$ cup vegetable oil
2 teaspoons Worcestershire sauce
$^1/_2$ teaspoon garlic powder
$^1/_2$ cup Burgundy wine
$^1/_2$ teaspoon white pepper
1 tablespoon lemon juice
$^1/_2$ teaspoon Louisiana hot sauce
2 tablespoons beer
$^1/_4$ cup corn syrup
1 large round steak, cut into $^1/_2$-inch strips

Mix all the ingredients together in a large glass bowl, cover, and marinate in the cooler for 4 hours. Place meat strips on grill, and cook until done as desired.

Cousin Pete's Peppered Porterhouse

I large porterhouse steak
$^1/_4$ cup **Worcestershire sauce**
3 teaspoons cracked black pepper
I thick-sliced green bell pepper
I thick-sliced onion
Thick-sliced whole mushrooms
2 teaspoons seasoned salt

Rub the porterhouse with Worcestershire sauce and cracked black pepper, and place in the cooler for 30 minutes.

Sauté the sliced green peppers, onions, and mushrooms in butter and season the veggies with seasoned salt. Grill the steak to your liking, and cover with the sautéed veggies. Serve with homemade steak sauce.

Filet Mirums

6 beef tenderloin steaks
$^3/_4$ cup dark rum
$^3/_4$ teaspoon garlic salt
$^1/_2$ cup finely chopped shallots
2 tablespoons lime juice
$^3/_4$ teaspoon red pepper
I tablespoon diced parsley
4 tablespoons butter

In a glass dish, combine $^1/_4$ cup rum, $^1/_4$ teaspoon garlic salt, $^3/_4$ cup shallots, 1 tablespoon lime juice, and $^1/_4$ teaspoon red pepper. Add the steaks, cover, and let rest for 60 minutes, turning twice. In a saucepan, simmer remaining rum, shallots, lime juice, parsley, and pepper with the butter. Brush the steak with the butter sauce, and grill for about 15 minutes, turning twice and basting with butter sauce.

Burgers LaGrange

10 hamburger buns
3 pounds ground beef
1/2 teaspoon white pepper
1 teaspoon garlic salt
1 teaspoon dried thyme
3 teaspoons parsley flakes
1/4 cup sour cream

In a large mixing bowl, combine the beef, pepper, garlic salt, thyme, parsley flakes, and sour cream. Mix well, and shape into 10 hamburger patties. Grill uncovered for about 5 minutes on each side until the meat is no longer pink on the inside. Serve with lettuce, tomato, and onion.

Austin Beer Steaks

2 large flank steaks
1 cup chili sauce
1/2 cup beer
1/3 cup vegetable oil
1/4 cup minced onion
1/4 cup minced cilantro
3 tablespoons red chili powder
1 teaspoon cumin
1/4 teaspoon garlic salt
1 teaspoon red pepper flakes
1 teaspoon Accent

In a mixing bowl, combine the chili sauce, beer, vegetable oil, onion, cilantro, chili powder, cumin, garlic salt, and red pepper flakes. Refrigerate the steaks for 8 hours in a large zip-top plastic bag with seasonings.

Remove the steaks from the marinade, shaking off any excess, and discard the remaining marinade from bag. Place the steaks on a well-oiled grill grid. Grill the steaks for about 25 minutes, covered loosely with foil. Turn the steaks twice during the cooking period. Let the steaks rest for 5 minutes before slicing the meat across the grain. Salt and pepper to taste.

Grand Pappy's Grillin' Steak

1 large steak cut of your choice
$^1/_4$ cup dark beer
12 ounces bottled mesquite with lime juice marinade
1 tablespoon garlic powder
$^1/_2$ teaspoon minced parsley
1 teaspoon Accent
2 teaspoons ground black pepper

In a resealable plastic bag, combine the marinade and seasonings. Set aside $^1/_2$ cup of marinade mixture for brushing on during cooking. Add the steak to the bag; seal and toss bag around with your hands so that the steak is completely covered with marinade. Marinate in the refrigerator for 6 hours.

Remove the steak from the bag; discard used marinade. Grill until desired texture is reached, brushing every 5 minutes with the remaining marinade.

Old Wishbone's Chuck Wagon Grillin' Meat

1 shot bourbon
$^1/_2$ cup chopped onion
$^1/_2$ cup lemon juice
$^1/_4$ cup vegetable oil
$^1/_2$ teaspoon seasoned salt
$^1/_2$ teaspoon celery salt
$^1/_2$ teaspoon black pepper
$^1/_2$ teaspoon oregano
$^1/_2$ teaspoon thyme
$^1/_2$ teaspoon rosemary
2 minced garlic cloves
1 large porterhouse steak, trimmed of fat

Mix all the ingredients except meat for marinade. In a glass dish, marinate the steak for 6 hours, turning several times and basting with marinade. Cook on the grill for 10 minutes on each side, or until steak reaches the texture you desire.

Drunken Swiss Burgers

2 pounds lean ground beef
$1/4$ cup homemade steak sauce
$1/4$ cup beer
I large thick-sliced sweet onion
4 slices Swiss cheese
4 whole wheat rolls, split
Lettuce

In a small saucepan, combine the steak sauce and beer, and simmer for about 3 minutes; set aside. Shape the ground beef into 4 large patties. Place the onion slices on the grill, and cook, uncovered, for about 5 minutes. Add patties; continue to grill, uncovered, for about 15 minutes, or until the onions are tender and the hamburger centers are no longer pink, turning every 5 minutes. Baste the burgers generously with the beer sauce about 3 minutes before the burgers are finished, top with the cheese. Line the bottom half of each roll with lettuce. Top each burger with grilled onion and beer sauce.

Willy and Waylon BBQ Ribs

5 pounds trimmed beef ribs
3 tablespoons butter
$^1/_4$ cup minced celery
$^1/_2$ cup minced onion
1 teaspoon minced garlic
$^1/_2$ cup tomato puree
2 tablespoons brown sugar
3 tablespoons apple cider vinegar
$^1/_4$ cup beef stock
2 tablespoons Worcestershire sauce
$^1/_2$ teaspoon white pepper
$^1/_2$ teaspoon cayenne
1 bay leaf
$^1/_2$ teaspoon chili powder
$^1/_2$ teaspoon cumin
1 tablespoon Accent

In a large saucepan, melt the butter and sauté celery, onion, and garlic for about 12 minutes or until all are tender and soft. Add the tomato puree, brown sugar, vinegar, beef stock, Worcestershire sauce, peppers, bay leaf, chili powder, cumin, and Accent; simmer 25 minutes, stirring every 3 minutes so the sauce doesn't scorch.

Cool for 20 minutes, discard the bay leaf, and cover and refrigerate the sauce for 2 hours. Preheat the grill with coals, and then add hickory wood chunks. Place the ribs on the grill, and brown both sides, baste with sauce, and close grill lid. Cook for about 30 minutes, turning and basting ribs every 5 minutes. Note: The ribs will be very dark on the outside, but tasty as heck!

Red Eye—Rib Eyes

8 thick-cut rib eye steaks
I teaspoon ground cumin
2 tablespoons vegetable oil
$^1/_2$ cup chopped pickled jalapeño peppers
$^1/_2$ cup chopped parsley

Combine the chopped jalapeños and parsley in a mixing bowl. Cut a pocket in the side of each steak without cutting all the way through. Pack the pockets with the jalapeño mixture and close pockets with toothpicks.

Combine the remaining ingredients, and rub all sides of steaks to cover well. Let the steaks cool in the fridge for 1 hour. Grill the steaks for 15 minutes, turning twice. Remove the toothpicks, and serve.

I Don't Think Hank Done It This Away Roast

3-pound beef chuck roast
$^1/_3$ cup whiskey
$^1/_2$ cup dark brown sugar
$^1/_3$ cup soy sauce
$^1/_3$ cup beer
I tablespoon Worcestershire sauce
I tablespoon lemon juice
I teaspoon garlic salt

Combine the whiskey, brown sugar, soy sauce, beer, Worcestershire sauce, lemon juice, and garlic salt; mix together well. Place the chuck roast into a large zip-top plastic bag; add all but 1 cup of the whiskey marinade, and seal. Refrigerate for 8 hours, turning every 2 hours to coat all sides of the roast. Grill for about an hour, turning and basting with reserved marinade every 30 minutes. Let the cooked roast stand for 20 minutes before slicing into thin cuts of meat.

Lancaster Mustard Ribs

5-pound beef rib rack
1 tablespoon mustard seed
2 tablespoons Dijon mustard
1 teaspoon garlic salt
1 teaspoon white pepper
2 tablespoons soft honey
1 package roast beef gravy with mushrooms

Place the roast on the grill, and cook for 20 minutes. Meanwhile, mix together the mustard seed, Dijon mustard, garlic salt, pepper, and honey. Remove the roast from the grill, and spread half the mustard sauce over both sides of the roast. Cook the roast uncovered for another 35 minutes or so, turning and basting with mustard sauce every 15 minutes. Remove cooked roast from grill, and cover with foil. Cook the gravy as to package instructions, and serve over slices of cooked roast.

Sticks in My Rump

1 large rump steak, cubed
10 ounces whole mushrooms
1 diced red pepper
1 diced green pepper
1 diced yellow pepper
1 chunked white onion
Olive oil for brushing
1 tablespoon seasoning salt

Thread the steak cubes onto metal skewers alternating with the vegetables. Brush the kebabs with the olive oil. Place over hot coals for about 5 minutes, turning and basting until desired texture. Sprinkle with seasoning salt, and serve.

The Classic Bacon Grilled Cheeseburger

6 slices thick-cut smoked bacon
2 pounds ground chuck steak
Salt
Pepper
Garlic powder
6 slices sharp cheddar cheese
6 split hamburger buns topped with sesame seeds
Butter
6 crisp lettuce leaves
6 slices tomato
Yellow mustard
Tomato ketchup
Real mayonnaise

In a skillet, brown the bacon until crisp, drain on paper towels, and set aside. Shape the ground chuck into 6 patties, and season both sides with salt, pepper, and garlic powder. Grill the patties for about 10 minutes, turning once. Top the patties with cheese slices during the last minute of grilling, closing the grill lid so cheese can melt. Butter the bun slices and toast on grate for 30 seconds.

Serve the cheese burgers hot on the toasted buns with lettuce, tomato, bacon, mustard, ketchup, and mayonnaise.

Otter Island Sizzling Beach Steaks

4 large tenderloin steaks
2 teaspoons dried basil
1 teaspoon crushed dried tarragon
1 teaspoon dried chives
$^1/_4$ teaspoon cumin
4 minced garlic cloves

Combine the basil, tarragon, chives, cumin, and garlic cloves. Rub the herbs onto both sides of the steaks, pressing hard into the surface of the meat to allow penetration. Grill the steaks for about 10 minutes, turning once during grilling time.

Her Majesty's Grilled Steak

1 large sirloin
1/3 cup vinegar
1/3 cup vegetable oil
3 tablespoons brown sugar
2 tablespoons Worcestershire sauce
2 crushed garlic cloves
2 sliced sweet onions
1 tablespoon Accent
1 teaspoon white pepper

Place the onions on the bottom and top of the steaks in a glass dish. Mix the remaining ingredients together; pour over steak. Cover the dish, and marinate the steaks in the refrigerator for 8 hours. Grill the steak for about 20 minutes, turning once. Salt and pepper to taste, and serve after letting the steak rest for 5 minutes.

Atlanta Grilled Roast

5-pound beef loin
1 tablespoon minced garlic
2 teaspoons minced rosemary
2 teaspoons Accent
1/2 teaspoon white pepper
1/4 teaspoon cayenne

Trim the roast of any excess fat. Combine the garlic, rosemary, Accent, white pepper, and cayenne together, and rub into all sides of the roast. Place the roast in the cooler, wrapped in plastic, for 24 hours.

Slowly grill the roast until the center reaches 130 degrees, turning every 30 minutes. Let the roast rest for 30 minutes before slicing.

Pennsylvania Pride Grilled Steak and Cream

8 large sirloin steaks trimmed of any excess fat
20 ounces chopped green onions
I tablespoon minced garlic
I tablespoon coarse ground black pepper
2 tablespoons brandy
I pint cream
2 ounces butter

Press the coarse ground black pepper into all sides of the steaks. Melt the butter in a large pan and fry the onions and garlic until all is soft. Stir in the cream and bring to a boil, stirring often. Add the brandy and salt and pepper to taste. Grill the peppered steaks for about 10 minutes or according to taste. To serve, let the steaks rest for 5 minutes, and top each steak with the cream sauce.

Littlerock BBQ Rump Steaks

4 large rump steaks, trimmed of excess fat
14 crushed black peppercorns
¹/₄ pint ketchup
¹/₄ cup beer
2 tablespoons brown sugar
2 tablespoons soy sauce
I tablespoon cider vinegar
I ounce butter
I tablespoon vegetable oil
I teaspoon minced parsley
I tablespoon Accent

Press the peppercorns well into both sides of the steaks and place the steaks in the cooler. In a saucepan, combine the ketchup, beer, brown sugar, soy sauce, vinegar, butter, vegetable oil, parsley, and Accent; bring to a boil. Grill the steaks for about 10 to 12 minutes or according to taste. To serve, let the steaks rest for 5 minutes, top each steak with the BBQ sauce, and serve hot.

Burgers Al Capone

2 pounds ground sirloin
1 chopped yellow onion
12 diced green onions
$^1/_2$ teaspoon liquid hickory smoke
$^1/_2$ cup dry red wine
$^1/_2$ teaspoon cumin
$^1/_2$ teaspoon Italian seasoning
$^1/_2$ cup Italian breadcrumbs
3 tablespoons butter
2 teaspoons sugar
1 sliced red onion
1 sliced tomato
Hamburger buns, split

In a mixing bowl, combine ground sirloin, half the yellow onions, half the green onions, liquid smoke, dry red wine, cumin, Italian seasoning, and breadcrumbs. Mix all the ingredients together well, and form into 8 patties. Refrigerate, covered with plastic, for 2 hours.

In a small saucepan, sauté the remaining yellow onions, green onions, 3 tablespoons butter, 3 tablespoons red wine, and 2 teaspoons sugar. Simmer until the onions start to caramelize. Grill the sirloin burgers for about 10 minutes, turning once. Serve the burgers in buns with sliced red onions, sliced tomato, and caramelized onions. Salt and pepper to taste.

Ribs Over Rhode Island

5 pounds beef back ribs
2 tablespoons soy sauce
$^1/_2$ cup chili sauce
$^1/_4$ cup rice wine
3 crushed garlic cloves
1 teaspoon ginger
2 tablespoons Accent
4 tablespoons minced cilantro
1 tablespoon onion powder

In a large bowl, combine the soy sauce, chili sauce, rice wine, garlic, ginger, Accent, cilantro, and onion powder. Place the ribs in a large shallow glass dish; pour the marinade over ribs. Cover with foil, and marinate in the refrigerator for 8 hours, turning twice.

Drain the ribs from marinade, and wrap them in foil. Cook the ribs on grill for about 20 minutes, turning twice. Using potholders, remove the ribs from foil, and place back on hot grill. Grill the ribs for another 10 minutes turning twice, and basting with leftover marinade. Let the ribs rest for 10 minutes before slicing and serving.

Hot Hickory Hills Grilled Steak

3 tablespoons lime juice

1 tablespoon lemon juice

1 tablespoon garlic powder

1 chopped and seeded jalapeño pepper

$^1/_4$ cup chopped sweet onion

1 tablespoon hickory liquid smoke

1 cup homemade steak sauce

1 thick round steak, trimmed of excess fat

In a large food processor or blender, combine the lime juice, lemon juice, garlic powder, pepper, onion, liquid smoke, and homemade steak sauce; cover and blend until the sauce is very smooth.

Place the steak in a large shallow glass dish and pour marinade over all. Cover with plastic wrap, and let the steak rest in the refrigerator for 2 hours. Place the steak on the grill, and cook for about 20 minutes, turning twice. Let the steak rest for 10 minutes before slicing. Serve with more of your homemade steak sauce.

Crazy Eyes Crandle's New York Strips

4 large New York strip steaks

1 teaspoon cayenne

2 tablespoons whole coffee beans

2 tablespoons whole black peppercorns

Melted butter

Garlic salt with parsley

Coarsely grind the cayenne, coffee beans, and peppercorns in a grinder. Make score marks into the steaks, and rub ground mixture into all sides of the steaks. Let the steaks rest in the cooler for 30 minutes, wrapped in plastic. Remove them from the cooler, and rub them down with melted butter. Lightly season the steaks with garlic salt, and grill for about 15 minutes, turning once. Allow the steaks to rest for 5 minutes before serving.

WOODS FOR SMOKING

If you're gonna be a famous outdoor cook, you gotta know your characteristics of grilling and smokin' woods. And guess what? Your old cousin Rick's gonna help ya out!

Alder: Great for salmon, fish, shellfish, and poultry. This tree originates on the West Coast of the United States and generally produces a light, delicate to sweet, mild taste. It is the traditional wood used for smoking salmon, particularly in the Pacific Northwest. Alder wood works well on almost any fish.

Apple: Great for chicken, turkey, fish, and ham. This tree indigenous to the Northwest United States produces a mild and fruity type of taste. Many cooks say that it makes meat taste slightly sweet and fruity. It is mild enough for chicken and turkey. It may also be used for a great flavor for ham.

Cherry: Great for salmon, fish, shellfish, and poultry. Cherry produces a taste similar to apple, a very mild and fruity flavor. You will probably find the meat tasting somewhat sweet as well. If you can find cherry, it will be mild enough for chicken, turkey, and fish. I use cherry also for a great-tasting ham.

Hickory: Great for red meats, all ribs, and poultry. It has been said that hickory is the king of smoking woods, and it is prevalent in the South. Care should be used when cooking with this wood. It will produce a sweet to strong, hearty taste. Hickory is perfect for ribs and pork shoulders. It also enhances any red meat or poultry.

Maple: Great for poultry, ham, and vegetables. Maple is generally located in the Northeast United States. It is mildly smoky and mates well with poultry, ham, and vegetables. It will produce a sweet and light taste.

Mesquite: Great for chicken, beef, and fish. Extra care needs to be used with this mystical wood. Over the past decade, it has gained favor in cooking fajitas. The flavor can become strong very quickly. It is best used for grilling, where the smoke does not actually penetrate the meat. Small portions may be used when smoking, if other wood is the primary heat source.

Oak: Great for briskets, roasts, chops, and steaks. Oak is an excellent wood for smoking large pieces of meat for great lengths of time. You will find it assertive but always pleasant. Oak is probably the most versatile of all hardwoods. The smoke flavor goes exceptionally well with brisket.

Pecan: Great for briskets, roasts, chops, steaks, fish, and poultry. Located in abundance in the Southwest, this wood produces a medium fruity taste and is the choice of many professional cooks. Pecan will burn cool and offer a richness of character.

Never use pine, spruce, or other evergreen wood. Only use hardwoods for smoking and grilling.

CHAPTER SIX

GRILLIN' WITH POULTRY

I said it before, and I'll say it again! Poultry's just a fancy word for chicken! Poultry is both versatile and great on the grill. Whether you choose chicken, duck, or turkey, the trick is to simply marinate your poultry in a tangy marinade or use a dry rub with exotic spices for a variety of international flavors. With that said, let's get grillin' with yardbird!

Get Back Jack Grilled Chicken Breasts

4 chicken breasts with ribs
I tablespoon hot sauce
2 tablespoons bourbon
2 teaspoons ginger
I teaspoon allspice
$^1/_4$ cup chopped pecans
4 minced garlic cloves
2 tablespoons maple syrup
3 tablespoons homemade BBQ sauce
$^1/_2$ cup crushed pineapple
Olive oil

In a large glass bowl, combine the hot sauce, bourbon, ginger, allspice, pecans, cloves, maple syrup, BBQ sauce, and crushed pineapple. Stir well, and cover in the cooler for 8 hours, stirring every 2 hours.

Rub the chicken breasts on all sides with olive oil, and place on grill. Cook until the center of the meat reaches 165 degrees. Start basting the chicken breasts with the sauce during the last 5 minutes of cooking.

The Holland Grill Beer Butt Chicken

I large whole fryer chicken
2 teaspoons freshly ground black pepper
2 tablespoons Creole seasoning
I teaspoon cayenne
2 tablespoons garlic powder with parsley
I 12-ounce can of beer

To make the rub, combine the black pepper, Creole seasoning, cayenne, and garlic powder in a bowl, and mix well. Sprinkle a healthy amount of rub over the whole chicken, both inside and out.

Insert the can of beer into the cavity of the chicken, open end up, and carefully place the seasoned chicken with the beer can inside on the Holland grill. Cook for about 3 hours, and serve hot.

Mike Hoffman's Keystone-Style Game Hens

1 teaspoon seasoning salt
1 teaspoon garlic powder
1 teaspoon red chili pepper
1 cup apple jelly
1 cup ketchup
2 tablespoons cider vinegar
1 teaspoon red chili powder
6 Cornish game hens

In a mixing bowl combine the seasoning salt, garlic powder, and chili pepper. Rub the game hens inside and out with this mix. In another bowl, combine the jelly, ketchup, vinegar, and red chili powder and mix well.

Place the seasoned hens on the grill, and cook for about an hour, or until the meat is tender. Baste the hens with the sauce from the second bowl 20 minutes before the meat is done cooking.

Myrtle Beach-Style Beer Butt Chicken

1 large whole chicken
1 teaspoon Accent
1 tablespoon seasoning salt
1 can beer
1 tablespoon orange marmalade
1 tablespoon horseradish sauce

Season the chicken the night before cooking with the Accent and seasoning salt, and store in the refrigerator until ready for cooking. When the grill is ready, place the opened beer can on the grill. Place the chicken on the beer can. Close grill lid, and cook at 225 degrees for about 3 hours, or until the bird reaches 195 degrees.

Mix the orange marmalade and horseradish sauce together, and glaze chicken after the first hour.

When the chicken is done cooking, remove from grill, discard any remaining beer, and cut up the chicken to serve.

Hot-to-Trot Chicken

1 pound boneless skinless chicken breast halves
2 teaspoons chopped rosemary
2 tablespoons crushed black peppercorns
1/4 teaspoon cayenne

Combine the chopped rosemary, crushed peppercorns, and cayenne in a bowl. Press this mixture into both sides of the chicken breasts. Grill for about 5 minutes on each side of seasoned halves, or until the chicken is cooked throughout.

Hampton Game Hens

5 large Cornish hens
1 cup red raspberries
1 cup cider vinegar
3 tablespoons lime juice
1 tablespoon minced garlic
2 tablespoons chopped mint
1 teaspoon Accent
3/4 cup light olive oil

In a bowl, combine the red raspberries, cider vinegar, lime juice, minced garlic, chopped mint, Accent, and olive oil. Split the hens down the center to flatten, and place them in a shallow glass dish. Pour the sauce on top of the split hens, and let stand for 6 hours in the cooler. Grill, skin side down, for 15 minutes. Turn, and continue cooking for about 25 minutes, basting every 5 minutes with the sauce. Serve with any remaining sauce.

Nashville Charcoaled Chicky Bird

6 chicken broiler halves
2 tablespoons Accent
2 tablespoons garlic salt
1 tablespoon lemon pepper
1 cup lemon juice
3 tablespoons Worcestershire sauce
³/₄ cup butter

Sprinkle the chicken halves on both sides with Accent, garlic salt, and lemon pepper. Place the seasoned halves in a large glass dish. Mix the lemon juice and Worcestershire sauce, and add to the chicken dish. Marinate for 12 hours, turning every 4 hours. Light the charcoal, dot the chicken with butter, and bake the chicken dish in the oven at 230 degrees for 60 minutes. When the coals are good and gray, place the chicken halves on the grill, bone side down. Cook with grill lid closed for about 35 minutes, basting with marinade from dish every 10 minutes.

Chopper's BBQ Chicken

4 tablespoons white Worcestershire sauce
4 tablespoons ground pepper
4 tablespoons sugar
1 tablespoon Accent
¹/₂ cup lemon juice
¹/₂ cup cider vinegar
3 cups mayonnaise
5 pounds chicken breast halves, skinned, with bone

In a large bowl, combine the first 7 ingredients, cover, and chill for 3 hours. Place the chicken breasts in a shallow dish, and pour 2 cups of the sauce over them. Cover, and marinate the chicken in the refrigerator for 12 hours. Remove the chicken from the sauce, discarding old sauce. Grill the chicken for about 45 minutes with the grill lid closed, turning every 20 minutes. Heat the remaining sauce, and serve with the grilled chicken. Serve hot.

Jack Daniels Bird of Bourbon

I teaspoon garlic salt
I teaspoon white pepper
I teaspoon Dijon mustard
4 minced garlic cloves
3 tablespoons lemon juice
$^1/_2$ cup wine vinegar
3 tablespoons Worcestershire sauce
I cup ketchup
$^2/_3$ cup dark brown sugar
$^3/_4$ cup Jack Daniels
8 large skinless chicken breasts

Combine the first 10 ingredients in a large bowl, and mix well. Grill the chicken breasts for about 45 minutes with the grill lid closed. Start basting the chicken with the sauce during the last 20 minutes of grilling. Serve the grilled chicken with any remaining sauce. Serve hot.

Contraband Chicken

2 cups chili sauce
I cup red wine vinegar
2 tablespoons prepared horseradish
I tablespoon minced garlic
I teaspoon Accent
I teaspoon salt
$^1/_2$ teaspoon white pepper
6 bone-in chicken breast halves

In a large mixing bowl, combine the first 7 ingredients, and reserve half of the sauce. Add the chicken breast to the bowl and turn to coat. Cover, and marinate the chicken for 30 minutes in the refrigerator. Remove the chicken from the marinade, and grill for about 40 minutes, turning and basting often with the reserved marinade. Warm any reserved marinade, and serve with grilled chicken. Serve while hot.

Crazy Eye's Chicken

5 tablespoons melted butter

I tablespoon Cajun spice

2 cups vegetable oil

I tablespoon minced red chilies

I tablespoon chili powder

I tablespoon Accent

I teaspoon coriander

I teaspoon garlic salt

$^{1}/_{2}$ cup red wine vinegar

$^{1}/_{2}$ cup chipped cilantro

I tablespoon minced garlic

2 tablespoons Dijon mustard

8 bone-in chicken breasts

In a large bowl, mix the first 12 ingredients together, and pour over the chicken breast. Cover the chicken, and let marinate in the refrigerator for 8 hours. Remove the chicken from the marinade, and grill with the lid closed for about 40 minutes, turning every 10 minutes. Serve hot off the grill.

Cheezy Chicken

I cup homemade BBQ sauce

16 slices thick-cut bacon

8 American cheese cubes (I inch thick)

8 boneless, skinless chicken breast halves

Preheat the grill. Place the cheese in the center of the chicken breast. Fold the chicken around the cheese, and wrap 2 slices of bacon crisscross around the chicken. Secure with wooden tooth-picks. Grill on a well oiled rack for about 45 minutes, turning every 20 minutes until the chicken is tender. Brush with homemade BBQ sauce the last 15 minutes of grill time.

Augusta Smoked Chicken

4 whole chickens, cut in halves
I cup Italian-style salad oil
¹/₂ cup vegetable oil
6 tablespoons vinegar
3 tablespoons Worcestershire sauce
I teaspoon white pepper
3 tablespoons lemon juice
I teaspoon Accent
I teaspoon smoked salt

In a large glass dish, combine the salad oil, vegetable oil, vinegar, Worcestershire sauce, white pepper, lemon juice, Accent, and smoked salt. Marinate the chicken halves for 4 hours in the cooler. Place the chicken halves on the smoker, placing the drained marinade in the bottom of the pan. Add hickory chips to the coals and smoke for about 6 hours.

Las Vegas Hair of the Dog Chicken

I quart spicy tomato juice
I pint vodka
I tablespoon garlic salt
I tablespoon Accent
I tablespoon white pepper
I tablespoon Tabasco sauce
2 tablespoons lemon juice
2 tablespoons Worcestershire sauce
I tablespoon onion powder
I tablespoon celery seed
I tablespoon olive oil
6 skinless, boneless chicken breasts

Combine the first 11 ingredients, and pour off one glass full to taste. If all is good, and by the time you finish your glass it should be, pour marinade into a large dish with the chicken breasts. Cover, and marinate for 24 hours. Grill the chicken breasts with the lid closed for about 7 minutes per side. Serve hot.

Saturday Night at Harvey's Chicken

8 chicken breast halves with bone
1 cup chopped white onions
3 tablespoons Worcestershire sauce
7 tablespoons prepared horseradish
2 teaspoons white pepper
1 teaspoon garlic salt
³/₄ cup honey
³/₄ cup Dijon mustard
³/₄ cup beer

In a large pot, simmer the onions, Worcestershire sauce, horse-radish, pepper, garlic salt, honey, Dijon mustard, and beer. Grill the chicken while sauce is simmering. When the chicken is finished grilling, add to the sauce, and simmer for another 5 minutes. Serve hot.

Amigo's Chicken

1 large whole cut fryer chicken
1-ounce package taco seasoning mix
16-ounce can of tomato sauce
2 tablespoons olive oil
1 teaspoon garlic salt
3 tablespoons lemon juice
¹/₂ cup beer

In a large glass dish, combine the taco seasoning, tomato sauce, olive oil, garlic salt, lemon juice, and beer. Mix well, and place the chicken into the sauce. Marinate, covered in the refrigerator, for 6 hours, turning chicken pieces every 2 hours. Grill the chicken for about 45 minutes. Serve hot.

Rose Bowl Party Chickens

5 tablespoons butter
2 tablespoons honey
4 teaspoons chili powder
$1/2$ teaspoon cayenne
1 teaspoon marjoram
2 minced garlic cloves
3 tablespoons orange juice
$1/4$ teaspoon garlic salt
$1/4$ teaspoon white pepper
2 Cornish hens, halved lengthwise

In a saucepan, melt the butter with honey, chili powder, cayenne, marjoram, and garlic. Remove the pan from the heat, and stir in the juice, garlic salt, and pepper. Grill the hen halves, skin sides down for about 6 minutes. Turn the halves over, and grill for another 6 minutes. Baste the hens with the sauce for the last 5 minutes of cooking.

34 Raceway Chicken

1 large fryer chicken
2 quarts of water
$1/4$ cup pickling spice
$1/3$ cup salt

In a large stock pot, bring the water, pickling spice, and salt to a boil. Remove from the heat, and chill for 3 hours.

After the pickling water is chilled, add the whole chicken, and marinate in the refrigerator for 24 hours. Remove the chicken, and discard the pickling marinade. Dry the chicken and remove any excess pickling spice. Grill with the lid closed for about an hour, or until the center of the chicken reaches 185 degrees.

49 Panhead Grilled Chicken

3/4 **cup white vinegar**
1/2 **cup vegetable oil**
1/4 **cup beer**
4 crushed garlic cloves
3 tablespoons brown sugar
2 tablespoons Worcestershire sauce
2 teaspoons hot sauce
1/2 **teaspoon ground mustard seed**
2 pounds chicken pieces

Combine all the ingredients, except the chicken, and set aside.
Grill the chicken until the juices run clear when pierced with a fork.
Remove the chicken from grill, and coat each piece in the prepared
sauce. Return chicken to grill and cook for another 3 minutes on
each side. Serve chicken with any remaining sauce on the side for
dipping.

Cottager Grilled Chicken Breasts

1 cup fresh lime juice
1 tablespoon honey
3/4 **cup water**
1/2 **teaspoon freshly ground pepper**
1/2 **teaspoon ground thyme**
2 tablespoons vegetable oil
1 tablespoon grated ginger root
3 pounds boned and skinned chicken breast halves

Combine all the ingredients except the chicken in a blender.
Pour marinade over chicken, and let marinate in the refrigerator for
8 hours. Grill over hot coals, turning once, until done.

Dad Got the Turkey Drunk!

1 large whole turkey breast
2 cups bourbon
³/₄ cup red wine
¹/₂ cup cooking sherry
¹/₃ cup soy sauce
3 tablespoons vegetable oil
3 tablespoons white sugar
2 tablespoons chopped rosemary
¹/₃ cup honey
¹/₃ cup ketchup
2 tablespoons brown sugar

Place the turkey in a large bowl. Stir together 1 cup bourbon, the red wine, cooking sherry, soy sauce, vegetable oil, white sugar, and rosemary. Pour over the turkey, and seal. Marinate for 8 hours in the refrigerator. Remove the turkey from the marinade, and grill for about 13 minutes per pound. Stir together the remaining cup of bourbon, honey, ketchup, and brown sugar. Brush this glaze onto the turkey after about 45 minutes on the grill, and again when the turkey is finished cooking.

The Moser Boy's Cabin on the Lake Grilled Turkey

12-pound whole turkey
2 cups beer
3 tablespoons chicken bouillon powder
3 teaspoons garlic powder
2 teaspoons onion powder
1 teaspoon Accent
1 teaspoon poultry seasoning
1/2 teaspoon minced parsley
1 teaspoon paprika

Prepare the charcoals for grill for medium to high heat. Rinse the turkey, and pat dry. Place the turkey, breast side down, on rack over the hot coals. Sear the turkey on both sides until the skin is dark brown. In a roasting pan, mix together the beer, bouillon, garlic powder, onion powder, Accent, poultry seasoning, parsley, and paprika. Place the turkey breast side down in pan. Pour the marinade over the turkey back, cover tightly with foil, and place the bird on the grill. Cook for about 13 minutes per pound. When the turkey is done cooking, let it stand for 20 minutes before slicing.

Mess Tent Turkey

1 large boneless turkey breast, thawed
Olive oil for basting
1 tablespoon onion flakes
1 tablespoon garlic powder
$^1/_2$ teaspoon ground thyme
$^1/_4$ teaspoon cayenne
$^1/_4$ teaspoon anise seed
$^1/_4$ teaspoon ground cloves
$^1/_4$ teaspoon Accent
1 crushed bay leaf

Prepare the grill with mesquite chips. Brush the turkey with olive oil. Combine the remaining ingredients, and sprinkle over the turkey. Place the turkey on the grill. Cover grill, and cook about 15 minutes per pound. Wrap the finished grilled turkey in foil, and let stand for 20 minutes before carving to serve.

Cousin Rick's Beach Burgers

1 pound turkey burger
$^1/_2$ cup butter saltine crumbs
10-ounce package frozen chopped spinach, thawed and drained
1 cup chopped white onion
$^1/_4$ teaspoon garlic salt
$^1/_3$ cup Dijon mustard, divided
$^1/_4$ cup roasted red peppers, sliced
4 slices mozzarella cheese
4 toasted kaiser rolls

In a large bowl, combine the turkey burger, saltine crumbs, drained spinach, onion, garlic salt, and $^1/_4$ cup of the Dijon mustard. Form into 4 patties. Cover, and chill the patties for 60 minutes. Grill the turkey burgers for about 10 minutes on each side. Top each burger with $1^1/_2$ teaspoons mustard, 1 tablespoon red pepper, and 1 slice of cheese. Cover, and grill until the cheese is good and melted. Serve on buttered, toasted kaiser rolls.

Mrs. Shirley Black's Holiday Grilled Turkey Breast

Large turkey breast with bone in
$^1/_2$ cup cherry preserves
1 tablespoon red wine vinegar
1 teaspoon Accent
1 teaspoon white pepper

Heat the grill to medium. Place the turkey skin side up on the rack over a drip pan. Cover, and grill the turkey for about 15 minutes per pound, or until the meat thermometer reads 175 degrees. In a bowl, combine the remaining ingredients, and brush the turkey with the glaze about 30 minutes before the turkey reaches the end of its grilling time. Let the turkey stand 20 minutes before carving.

Poker Night at Campbell's Grilled Turkey Wings

8 turkey wings
1 cup smooth peanut butter
1 cup water
1 cup beer
6 tablespoons soy sauce
6 tablespoons lemon juice
4 tablespoons brown sugar
6 chopped green onions
3 tablespoons hot sauce

Discard wing tips, and divide wings into 2 pieces. In a large saucepan, cover turkey wings with water and beer, and bring to a boil. Simmer for 25 minutes. Combine the remaining ingredients together to make the marinade, stirring well to dissolve the sugar. Remove the wings from the water, and place in marinade. Marinate the wings in the refrigerator for 12 hours. Remove from the marinade, and grill the wings over medium coals for about 30 minutes, turning every 5 minutes.

Smoke 'Em if You Got 'Em Turkey

I large whole turkey

Injection Marinade
$^1/_2$ cup vegetable oil
6 ounces beer
$^1/_2$ teaspoon cayenne

Turkey Paste (blended until smooth in food processor)
6 garlic cloves
I tablespoon ground black pepper
I tablespoon sea salt
I tablespoon peanut oil

Smoked Turkey Secret Mop
3 cups turkey stock
I cup water
12 ounces beer
$^1/_2$ cup olive oil
I tablespoon Accent

The night before smoking, inject the turkey with the injection marinade in all areas of the bird, injecting the most in the breast. Rub the turkey paste inside and out, including up under the skin as much as possible. Refrigerate the bird overnight in plastic wrap. The next day, wrap the turkey in wet cheesecloth, and smoke for $1^1/_2$ hours per pound at 220 degrees, breast side down, rewetting the cheesecloth every hour with water. After 6 hours, take off the cheesecloth and continue to cook, mopping with the smoked turkey secret mop every hour until the internal temperature reads 185 degrees. Let the finished smoked turkey rest for 20 minutes before carving.

Aimwell Grilled Turkey Breast

1 large boneless turkey breast
2 cups melted butter
1 cup Dijon mustard
1 cup shallots
2 teaspoons cilantro
$^1/_3$ cup chives
$^1/_2$ teaspoon white pepper
Peanut oil for basting

Combine the butter, mustard, shallots, cilantro, chives, and white pepper. Rub the turkey with peanut oil, and grill, turning every 30 minutes, until the internal temperature reaches 185 degrees. Baste the turkey with mustard sauce during the last 30 minutes of cooking time. Let the finished grilled turkey rest 20 minutes before slicing, and serve with any remaining mustard sauce.

Bobo Grilled Monster Wings

5 pounds turkey wings
32-ounce can of whole unpitted purple plums
5 tablespoons orange juice
4 tablespoons hoisin sauce
2 tablespoons soy sauce
2 teaspoons grated ginger
1 teaspoon white pepper
5 tablespoons toasted sesame seeds
1 tablespoon smoked salt

For the sauce, drain the plums, reserving the liquid. Pit plums. In a food processor, combine the pitted plums, reserved plum juice, orange juice, hoisin sauce, soy sauce, ginger, and pepper. Transfer the blended mixture to a saucepan. Bring to boiling; reduce heat. Simmer uncovered for about 20 minutes, and stir in the sesame seeds. Sprinkle the turkey wings with smoked salt and pepper, and place on grill. Cook the wings for about 40 minutes with the lid closed, turning them once. Brush them with the sauce often after the first 20 minutes of grilling. Heat any remaining sauce, and serve with the wings.

COUSIN RICK AND BUBBA

Cousin Rick and Bubba, two Iowa hicks, were driving down the road drinking a couple of bottles of beer on their way to Uncle Marvin's annual Barbecue Bash.

The passenger, Bubba, said, "Looky thar up ahead, Cousin Rick, it's a dadgum police roadblock! We're gonna get busted fer drinkin' these here beers!"

"Don't worry, Bubba," Cousin Rick said. "We'll just pull over and finish drinkin' these beers, then peel off the label and stick it on our foreheads, then throw the bottles under the truck seat."

"What fer?" asked Bubba.

"Just let me do the talkin', OK?" said Cousin Rick.

Well, they finished their beers, threw the empties out of sight, and put the labels on their foreheads. When they reached the roadblock, the sheriff said, "Howdy boys, ya'll been drinkin'?"

"No sir," said Cousin Rick while pointing at the labels. "Me and Bubba's on the patch."

CHAPTER SEVEN

GRILLIN' WITH LAMB

When grillin' with lamb, choose lamb that is light red with bones that are slightly pink rather than white. Remember that lamb is naturally fattier than other grillin' meats, so always trim the fat before placing it on your grill. This is a big cause of flareups.

Nancy's Lamb Kebabs

3 pounds boneless leg of lamb
2 teaspoons allspice
4 tablespoons lemon juice
1 teaspoon lime juice
¹/₄ cup olive oil
3 tablespoons Worcestershire sauce
¹/₂ cup chopped parsley
1 cup minced white onion
3 minced garlic cloves

Using a sharp knife, cut the lamb meat into 1-inch cubes. Place the meat in a large plastic bowl, and add the remaining ingredients. Turn the meat to coat well. Refrigerate the lamb in the bowl, covered, for 8 hours, turning every 2 hours. Skewer the meat cubes, and grill over coals for about 25 minutes, turning once.

Licking Lamb Chops

10 lamb loin chops
Salt and pepper to taste
1 tablespoon chopped mint
1 tablespoon thyme
1 tablespoon rosemary
1 teaspoon Accent
2 minced garlic cloves
1 cup fresh orange juice

Salt and pepper both sides of the chops. Combine the remaining ingredients in a bowl, and press into both sides of the chops. Grill for about 6 minutes per side, while basting with remaining sauce.

Bootleggin' Leg of Lamb

I large leg of lamb
3 tablespoons garlic salt with parsley
I teaspoon white pepper
4 minced garlic cloves
$1/2$ cup olive oil
I cup lemon juice

Mix all the marinade ingredients together, and store in the refrigerator for 24 hours in a covered bowl.

Brush the surface of the meat with the marinade, and then place the lamb in a large pan and cover with the remaining marinade. Cover, and marinate in the cooler for 16 hours. Place the meat on a spit, and cook for about 3 hours, turning every 20 minutes. Let the lamb rest for 15 minutes before carving.

Bungy Grilled Lamb Leg

I large leg of lamb, boned and trimmed of fat
I cup ketchup
I cup Worcestershire sauce
$1/4$ teaspoon Louisiana hot sauce
I teaspoon chili powder
I cup beer
$1/4$ cup dark brown sugar
I teaspoon celery salt
I teaspoon garlic salt with parsley
$1/2$ teaspoon white pepper

Combine the sauce ingredients in a large pan. Simmer, do not boil; remove from the stove, and allow to cool for 1 hour. Pour the sauce over the lamb leg, and marinate for 8 hours in the refrigerator or cooler. Grill for about 60 minutes, turning and basting every 20 minutes with remaining sauce.

Left Hand Bay Grilled Leg of Lamb

1 large leg of lamb, trimmed of fat
1 teaspoon salt
$^{1}/_{2}$ teaspoon pepper
$^{1}/_{2}$ teaspoon dried whole oregano
12 sliced garlic cloves
Hickory chips

Soak the hickory chips for 1 hour, drain, and set aside. Make several small cuts on the outside of the lamb meat, and stuff with the garlic slices. Rub the salt, pepper, and oregano over the surface of the lamb. Wrap the lamb in foil. Prepare the fire in a covered grill; sprinkle the hickory chips over the hot coals. Place the lamb on the grill, and grill for about 2 hours, turning every 30 minutes. Let the lamb stand, still wrapped in the foil, for 20 minutes before removing from foil and carving.

Contoocook Lamb Roast

1 large boneless lamb roast
2 sliced garlic cloves
2 sliced lemons
1 teaspoon garlic salt with parsley
$^{1}/_{2}$ teaspoon white pepper

Using a sharp knife, cut 6 evenly spaced openings on the roast, and stuff with garlic cloves. Rub the roast several times with the lemon slices, and dust with the garlic salt and pepper. Wrap the lamb in foil, and grill over medium coals with the lid closed for about 20 minutes per pound, or when the center of the lamb roast reads 175 degrees. Let the roast stand for 10 minutes before removing from the foil and slicing.

Three Forks Grilled Lamb Chops

8 thick-cut lamb chops
Salt and pepper to taste
4 halved garlic cloves
³/4 cup red wine vinegar
¹/2 cup olive oil
1 teaspoon rosemary

Sprinkle the chops on both sides with salt and pepper. Rub the garlic over the surface of the chops. Combine the red wine vinegar, olive oil, and rosemary, stirring well; baste the chops with the vinegar sauce, and set the remaining sauce aside. Grill the chops over medium coals for about 10 minutes per side. Baste often with the sauce while grilling.

Goobertown Chops

6 thick-cut lamb chops
¹/2 cup minced white onion
3 sliced garlic cloves
¹/4 cup light soy sauce
¹/3 cup cider vinegar
3 tablespoons honey
2 teaspoons ginger
¹/4 teaspoon dry mustard
¹/4 teaspoon white pepper

Place the chops in a large plastic container. Combine the remaining ingredients, and pour over the chops. Cover and refrigerate for 12 hours, turning every hour. Remove the chops from the marinade, reserving the remaining marinade. Grill for about 10 minutes per side, basting often with the remaining marinade while grilling.

Black Jack Grilled Leg of Lamb

I large leg of lamb, trimmed of fat
I tablespoon dry mustard
I teaspoon cardamom
$^1/_2$ teaspoon ground cloves
I tablespoon cider vinegar
$^3/_4$ cup apple juice
$^1/_2$ cup Dijon mustard
I tablespoon rosemary
2 teaspoons vegetable oil
I teaspoon garlic salt with parsley

In a large bowl, combine the dry mustard, cardamom, ground cloves, vinegar, apple juice, Dijon mustard, rosemary, vegetable oil, and garlic salt. Whisk well. Place the lamb leg in a large dish, and pour a third of the marinade over meat. Turn the meat several times to well coat. Cover the dish, and let rest in the cooler for 12 hours. Remove the lamb from the marinade, and grill for about 2 hours, turning and basting with remaining marinade every 15 minutes. Let the meat rest for 20 minutes before carving.

Bean Lake Station Grilled Rack of Lamb

I large rack of lamb ribs, trimmed of fat
$^3/_4$ cup olive oil
4 tablespoons chopped rosemary
2 teaspoons crushed red pepper
Salt and pepper to taste
Apple wood chips for cooking

Place the lamb ribs in a large glass dish. In a mixing bowl, combine the olive oil, rosemary, and crushed red pepper. Pour the marinade over the ribs, turning twice to coat well, cover, and let the meat marinate in the cooler for 24 hours. Drain the marinade from the ribs; sprinkle with salt and pepper, and grill for about 35 minutes over apple wood coals, turning every 10 minutes. Let the meat rest for 20 minutes before cutting between the bones to serve.

Loogootee Grilled Lamb

I leg of lamb, boned and butterflied
I cup chicken stock
$^1/_3$ cup of rum
$^1/_2$ cup lime juice
3 tablespoons dark brown sugar
I teaspoon allspice
$^1/_2$ teaspoon garlic salt
$^1/_2$ teaspoon pepper
2 minced garlic cloves
I cup sliced peaches with juice

Place the lamb meat in a large zip-top plastic bag. Add the remaining ingredients except the peaches and seal the bag. Marinate the meat for 12 hours in the refrigerator. Remove the lamb from the marinade, and place on the grill over medium heat; cook for about 20 minutes per side. Place the remaining marinade in a saucepan, and simmer until the mixture is reduced by about half. Slice the grilled lamb, and place on the serving tray with the peaches and drizzle with the heated marinade.

What Cheer BBQ Lamb Steaks

4 lamb steak cuts, trimmed of fat
I cup olive oil
4 tablespoons homemade **BBQ** sauce
2 tablespoons lemon juice

Combine the olive oil, BBQ sauce, and lemon juice in a shallow dish. Add the lamb steaks, and coat them in the mixture. Let marinate for 60 minutes. Grill the steaks for 5 minutes on each side, or to your liking. Let the steaks stand for 5 minutes before serving.

Bucksnort Lamb Ribs

1 rack of lamb, trimmed of fat
4 tablespoons stone-ground mustard
2 tablespoons Worcestershire sauce
1 teaspoon Accent
$^1/_2$ teaspoon crushed red pepper
3 minced garlic cloves

Place the lamb in a shallow glass dish. Combine the mustard, Worcestershire sauce, Accent, crushed red pepper, and minced garlic. Pour this mixture over the lamb, cover, and let marinate in the refrigerator for 24 hours. Remove the lamb rack from the marinade, and grill until the thermometer reads 150 degrees.

Sweet Lips Leg of Lamb

1 large leg of lamb, trimmed of fat, boned, and butterflied
2 cups spicy homemade BBQ sauce
1 teaspoon garlic powder
$^1/_4$ teaspoon white pepper
$^1/_4$ teaspoon smoked salt

In a nonmetal pan, spread the BBQ sauce over the lamb, season with garlic powder, pepper, and salt. Cover, and refrigerate for 8 hours, turning twice. Grill for about $2^1/_2$ hours, turning every 30 minutes and basting with sauce. Let the meat rest for 10 minutes before carving.

Bugtussle Grilled Lamb Chops

8 thick-cut lamb chops, trimmed of fat
$^1/_2$ cup lemon juice
$^1/_2$ cup olive oil
$^1/_2$ cup white wine
1 teaspoon crushed garlic
1 teaspoon salt
1 teaspoon dried rosemary
1 teaspoon white pepper
1 tablespoon red pepper flakes

Add all the marinade ingredients together, and pour over the chops. Cover, and refrigerate for 72 hours, turning twice every 4 hours. Grill with the lid closed for about 20 minutes on each side of the chops.

Cut-N-Shoot Grilled Chops

Large lamb loin chops
4 tablespoons olive oil
Salt and pepper to taste
$^1/_2$ cup jalapeño preserves

Brush the chops lightly with olive oil, season to taste with the salt and pepper. Grill the chops for about 5 minutes on each side. Warm the jalapeño preserves to room temperature, and serve with the grilled lamb chops, about 2 tablespoons per chop.

London Grilled Fillets

4 large lamb tenderloins, trimmed of fat
1 teaspoon crushed garlic
2 tablespoons lemon juice
4 teaspoons olive oil
$^1/_4$ teaspoon garlic salt
$^1/_4$ teaspoon white pepper

Place the fillets in a shallow dish, and add the garlic, lemon juice, olive oil, garlic salt, and white pepper. Cover the dish, and let stand for 60 minutes. Preheat the grill to medium. Place the fillets on the grill, and cook for 10 minutes, turning to cook on all sides. Let the fillets rest for 10 minutes before slicing and serving.

Sour Lake Grilled Lamb Chops

6 thick-cut shoulder blade lamb chops
1 cup fresh minced mint
$^1/_2$ cup white wine vinegar
3 tablespoons sugar
1 tablespoon water
1 tablespoon Accent
$^3/_4$ cup plain yogurt
2 minced garlic cloves

Mix all the ingredients together except the chops. Transfer 2 tablespoons into a bowl. Add 1 tablespoon water. Cover and chill. Cover the chops with the remaining marinade, and chill for 8 hours. Grill the chops over charcoal for 5 minutes on each side. Transfer to serving platter, and drizzle with reserved mint sauce.

Mosquitoville Leg of Lamb

1 large cut leg of lamb, boned and butterflied
$^1/_2$ cup olive oil
$^1/_4$ cup soy sauce
$^1/_4$ cup lemon juice
3 tablespoons Dijon mustard
$^1/_4$ teaspoon white pepper
2 tablespoons vermouth
3 chopped garlic cloves
1 tablespoon chopped rosemary

Remove all the fat from the leg of lamb. Combine all the remaining ingredients, and pour over the lamb. Marinate in the cooler for 6 hours, turning every hour to coat well. Bring the lamb to room temperature before grilling. Grill for about 20 minutes per side. Let the lamb rest for 10 minutes before carving.

Ronkonkoma Grilled Lamb

1 leg of lamb, boned
1 cup olive oil
1 cup lemon juice
4 crushed garlic cloves
2 bay leaves
6 sprigs parsley
2 tablespoons Accent
$^1/_2$ teaspoon white pepper
1 tablespoon dried sage
1 tablespoon dried thyme
1 tablespoon rosemary
$^1/_2$ cup beef broth
$^1/_2$ cup red wine
3 tablespoons chopped shallots
4 tablespoons butter

Remove all the fat from the leg of lamb. Combine the oil, lemon juice, garlic, bay leaves, parsley, Accent, pepper, $\frac{1}{2}$ tablespoon sage, $\frac{1}{2}$ tablespoon thyme, and $\frac{1}{2}$ tablespoon rosemary. Pour this marinade over the leg of lamb in a shallow glass dish, and marinate for 30 hours, turning every 6 hours. Drain the meat, and reserve the marinade. Grill the lamb on the spit for about 70 minutes. Combine the beef broth, wine, shallots, and remaining sage, rosemary, and thyme to the reserved marinade. Simmer the marinade for 1 hour, stirring often. Add the butter, and let it melt in the marinade. Pour the marinade over sliced lamb meat. Serve hot.

WHAT HERBS AND SPICES GO WITH WHAT?

Beef: basil, bay, chili, cilantro, curry, cumin, garlic, marjoram, mustard, oregano, parsley, pepper, rosemary, sage, savory, tarragon, and thyme.

Chicken: allspice, basil, bay, cinnamon, curry, dill, fennel, garlic, ginger, lemongrass, mustard, paprika, rosemary, saffron, sage, savory, tarragon, and thyme.

Corn: chili, curry, dill, marjoram, parsley, savory, and thyme.

Desserts: allspice, angelica, anise, cardamom, cinnamon, cloves, fennel, ginger, lemon peel, mace, nutmeg, mint, orange peel, and rosemary.

Fish and seafood: anise, basil, bay, cayenne, celery seed, chives, curry, dill, fennel, garlic, ginger, lemon peel, mustard, oregano, parsley, rosemary, thyme, saffron, sage, savory, tarragon, and marjoram.

Fruits: allspice, anise, cardamom, cinnamon, cloves, coriander, ginger, and mint.

Lamb: basil, bay, cinnamon, coriander, cumin, curry, dill, garlic, marjoram, mint, mustard, oregano, parsley, rosemary, savory, tarragon, and thyme.

Potatoes: basil, caraway, celery seed, chervil, chives, coriander, dill, marjoram, oregano, paprika, parsley, poppy seed, rosemary, tarragon, and thyme.

Tomatoes: basil, bay, celery seed, cinnamon, chili, curry, dill, fennel, garlic, ginger, gumbo file, lemongrass, marjoram, oregano, parsley, rosemary, savory, tarragon, and thyme.

CHAPTER EIGHT

GRILLIN' WITH FISH AND SEAFOOD

E ven though I live in Iowa, I always find ways to get my seafood fresh. As far as fish goes, the mighty Mississippi River is just a stone chuckin' from my back deck. Here are a few good tips on grillin' with fish and seafood.

Keep an eye on your catch! Fish and seafood cook really quickly on the grill. Always spray the cooking grate with spray oil before placing your fish and seafood on it. This will help you keep your fillets in check and not in your heat source. Turn your fish and seafood only once during the grilling process. Tuna and salmon can be grilled directly on the grate, but I highly recommend you use a basket for seafood such as catfish, snapper, and all shellfish.

Comfort Grilled Salmon

2 pounds salmon steaks
1 teaspoon garlic powder
$^{1}/_{2}$ teaspoon Accent
$^{1}/_{4}$ teaspoon seasoning salt
4 tablespoons olive oil
3 tablespoons white wine vinegar
$^{1}/_{2}$ cup lemon juice

Place all the marinade ingredients in a bowl, and mix well. Pour the marinade over the salmon steak, and chill for 3 hours, turning twice. Baste the salmon steaks while grilling with remaining marinade.

Walla Walla Tuna

5 thick-cut tuna steaks
$^{1}/_{2}$ teaspoon Accent
$^{1}/_{2}$ teaspoon sage
1 cup Italian-style salad oil
$^{1}/_{4}$ cup lemon juice

Place the steaks in a shallow glass dish. Mix together the Accent, sage, salad oil, and lemon juice. Pour over the tuna steaks, and chill in the refrigerator for 60 minutes. Grill for about 5 minutes on each side of steaks. Salt and pepper to taste.

Tijuana Grilled Shrimp

6 pounds large shrimp with shells on
I cup tequila
$^{1}/_{2}$ cup olive oil
$^{1}/_{4}$ cup chili sauce
$^{1}/_{4}$ cup lime juice

Combine all the marinade ingredients, and mix well. Pour over the shrimp, and let chill, covered, for 8 hours in the refrigerator. Grill the shrimp for about 3 minutes on each side.

Swashbuckler Swordfish

6 swordfish steaks, cut in halves
$^{1}/_{2}$ cup lemon juice
2 tablespoons Dijon mustard
$^{1}/_{2}$ cup light soy sauce
I tablespoon grated lemon peel
2 crushed garlic cloves
$^{1}/_{2}$ cup olive oil
Salt and white pepper to taste

Place the swordfish steaks in a shallow glass dish. Combine the marinade ingredients, and mix well. Pour the marinade over the steaks, and chill for 4 hours. Grill the steaks for about 5 minutes on each side. Salt and pepper to taste using white pepper.

Snappy Brown's Grilled Salmon Burgers

14 ounces canned salmon
2 tablespoons lemon juice
2 tablespoons Dijon mustard
³/₄ cup dry seasoned breadcrumbs
¹/₂ cup sliced green onions
3 egg whites

Drain and flake the salmon. Combine the lemon juice and mustard. Blend the flaked salmon with the breadcrumbs, green onions, and lemon juice mustard mixture. Mix in the egg whites, and blend well. Form the mixture into 4 patties, and grill on an oiled grate until the patties are golden brown. Serve with hamburger buns and your favorite condiments.

Sister Sibs Grilled Sablefish

1 large sablefish fillet
¹/₂ cup tomato sauce
3 tablespoons minced onion
1 tablespoon minced parsley
1 teaspoon Worcestershire sauce
¹/₄ teaspoon white pepper
¹/₄ teaspoon basil
¹/₄ teaspoon sugar
1 tablespoon olive oil
3 teaspoons lemon juice

Combine the tomato sauce, onion, parsley, Worcestershire sauce, pepper, basil, and sugar in a saucepan. Cook and simmer for 5 minutes, stirring often. Do not boil. Mix in the olive oil and lemon juice, and brush on to the sablefish. Wrap the sablefish in foil, and grill for about 15 minutes, turning once. Salt and pepper to taste.

Sucker Flats Grilled Shark

4 pounds shark steaks
4 tablespoons butter
2 cups chopped onions
2 minced garlic cloves
I cup beer
$^{1}/_{2}$ cup vinegar
4 tablespoons brown sugar
3 teaspoons Worcestershire sauce
I cup ketchup

Rinse the shark in cold water, and pat dry with paper towels. Set aside. Melt the butter in a medium saucepan. Add the onion and garlic; sauté until tender. Stir in the remaining ingredients. Bring mixture to a boil, stirring often. Reduce the heat, and simmer for 20 minutes, or until the sauce starts to thicken. Remove from heat. Baste the shark steaks with the sauce, and place on a well-oiled grill. Cook for 5 minutes. Baste and turn; cook another 5 minutes, or until the shark steaks flake easily with a grilling fork.

Road's End Grilled Lobster Tails

8 live lobsters
8 tablespoons butter
I cup lemon juice

Quickly immerse the lobsters headfirst into a pot of boiling water for 1 minute. Then snap off the tails. Using a large pair of shears, remove and discard the undershells of the tail sections. Insert skewers lengthwise through the hard shell at both ends to prevent curling. Put as many tails as will fit on each skewer. Place the lobsters shell side down on the grill grates, which should be set at the highest position on your grill. Grill for 5 minutes at medium heat. Turn, and grill the other side for 5 minutes, or until the meat is opaque. Return the lobster tails to the shell-side-down position, and baste the meat with the melted butter mixed with lemon juice.

Scuba Diver Grilled Lobsters

4 large lobsters
2 cups melted butter
Salt and white pepper to taste
8 slices of fresh lemon

In a large pot, boil about 4 gallons of water. Add one live lobster, and cover. Cook for 3 minutes. Remove the lobster with a large pair of tongs, and return the water to boiling. Do the same with the remaining 3 lobsters. Turn the lobsters upside down, and cut lengthwise from the tip of the tail through the head, using a large pair of sheers. This will give you 8 lobster halves. Place the lobsters shell side down on a medium hot grill, baste with butter, and sprinkle with salt and white pepper. Cover the grill, and cook for about 10 minutes, or until the meat at the thickest part of the tail turns opaque. Serve with melted butter and a slice of fresh lemon.

Wing Dam BBQ Walleye

4 pounds walleye fillets, cut in cubes for skewering
4 tablespoons soy sauce
4 tablespoons teriyaki sauce
2 tablespoons honey
2 tablespoons sesame seed oil
2 tablespoons Cajun spice
I teaspoon Worcestershire sauce
Salt and white pepper to taste
I sweet red pepper, sliced for skewering
I green pepper, sliced for skewering
I yellow pepper, sliced for skewering
4 small onions, cut in half

In a large bowl, combine the soy sauce, teriyaki sauce, honey, sesame seed oil, Cajun spice, Worcestershire sauce, and salt and pepper. Stir well and set aside. In a large shallow glass dish, place the red peppers, green peppers, yellow peppers, and onions, topped with the walleye cubes. Pour the marinade over all, and cover. Chill for 8 hours in the cooler. When ready to grill, put the fish, peppers, and onions on skewers and grill for about 6 minutes on each side with the lid closed.

Big Shrimpin' Baby

2 pounds jumbo shrimps, peeled and deveined
I pound sliced bacon
I cup homemade BBQ sauce
$^1/_2$ cup shredded cheddar cheese

Wrap each shrimp in a slice of bacon and thread into skewers to hold in place. Brush the shrimp with homemade barbecue sauce. Grill over hot coals until the bacon is good and crisp. Sprinkle with cheese just before the shrimp and bacon are finished cooking, and allow the cheese to melt. Serve hot and dip with remaining BBQ sauce.

Foiled Again Cod

2 pounds cod fillets
4 tablespoons butter
$^1/_2$ cup lemon juice
2 tablespoons chopped parsley
2 teaspoons garlic salt with parsley
$^1/_2$ teaspoon white pepper
$^1/_2$ teaspoon paprika
I cup minced onion

Place the cod fillets in heavy aluminum foil boats. Melt the butter, and then stir in the lemon juice, parsley, garlic salt, and white pepper. Pour the butter mixture over the fillets, sprinkle with paprika, and top with minced onion. Fold and seal the foil. Grill the wrapped fillets for 7 minutes per side. Let the fish stand wrapped in foil boats for 3 minutes before serving.

Good Morning Grilled Catfish

2 pounds catfish fillets
I tablespoon lemon juice
I tablespoon instant coffee
$^1/_2$ cup melted butter
$^1/_2$ teaspoon onion powder
$^1/_2$ teaspoon garlic salt with parsley

Combine the lemon juice, instant coffee, melted butter, onion powder, and garlic salt. Brush this mixture onto the catfish fillets. Grill on medium heat for about 10 minutes per side, brushing with sauce every 5 minutes.

Black-Eyed Nellie's Mississippi Catfish

4 catfish fillets
I teaspoon lemon pepper
I teaspoon white pepper
I teaspoon creole seasoning
I teaspoon blackened fish seasoning
I teaspoon Accent
3 tablespoons lemon juice

Combine the lemon pepper, white pepper, creole seasoning, blackened fish seasoning, and Accent. Sprinkle the fillets with the lemon juice and seasoning mixture on all sides. Spray a wire fish grilling basket with cooking spray; place the seasoned fillets in the basket. Grill the fillets, covered, for about 10 minutes on each side, or until the catfish flakes with a fork. Salt and pepper to taste, and serve hot from the grill.

White Meat Feller Grilled Catfish

8 whole cleaned catfish
¹/₂ cup melted butter
I cup lemon juice
¹/₄ teaspoon Louisiana hot sauce
I teaspoon prepared mustard
3 tablespoons Worcestershire sauce
I teaspoon garlic salt with parsley
I teaspoon white pepper
I teaspoon paprika

Combine all the ingredients except for the catfish, and blend well. Place the catfish on a well-oiled grate, and grill for 20 minutes on each side, basting with sauce every 5 minutes. Salt and pepper to taste, and serve hot.

Stonewall's Grilled Scallops

2 pounds large scallops
1 cup butter
1 cup chopped onions
3 chopped garlic cloves
$^1/_2$ cup lemon juice
$^1/_3$ cup chopped parsley
$^1/_4$ teaspoon sea salt

Melt the butter in a saucepan. Sauté the onion and garlic until both are soft. Remove from heat, and stir in the lemon juice, chopped parsley, and sea salt. Place the scallops in a bowl, and toss with the butter mixture. Let stand for 4 minutes. Thread the scallops onto skewers, and grill for about 5 minutes per side. Return the butter mixture to the saucepan, and bring to a boil. Reduce the heat to low, and toss the grilled scallops in sauce. Serve hot.

Rubicon Scallops

2 pounds fresh scallops
3 cups cherry tomatoes
3 cups mushrooms
20 ounces drained pineapple chunks
2 chopped green peppers
$^1/_2$ cup olive oil
$^1/_2$ cup lemon juice
$^1/_2$ cup chopped parsley
$^1/_2$ cup light soy sauce
1 teaspoon sea salt
$^1/_2$ teaspoon white pepper

Rinse the scallops with cold water to remove any remaining shell pieces. Place the scallops, tomatoes, mushrooms, pineapple chunks, and green peppers in a large glass bowl. Combine the olive oil, lemon juice, parsley, soy sauce, sea salt, and white pepper. Pour the sauce over the scallops, and let stand for 45 minutes, stirring every 10 minutes. Using long skewers, alternate the scallops, tomatoes, mushrooms, pineapple, and green peppers until the skewers are filled. Grill for about 5 minutes per side, basting with sauce.

Sand in My Britches Shrimp

1 pound large shrimp, shelled and deveined
1 cup Louisiana hot sauce
$^1/_3$ cup melted butter
2 ribs celery, cut into large pieces

Combine the Louisiana hot sauce and butter in a bowl. Alternately thread the shrimp and celery onto skewers. Place in a shallow bowl. Pour $^1/_3$ cup of sauce mixture over the kebabs. Cover; refrigerate for 50 minutes. Grill the shrimp for about 5 minutes, turning once. Heat the remaining sauce mixture, and pour over the cooked kebabs before serving.

Hammerhead Shrimp

$^1/_2$ cup homemade BBQ sauce
4 tablespoons orange juice
1 pound medium shrimp in shells
2 nectarines
2 yellow onions, cut into 8 wedges each

Stir together the homemade BBQ sauce and orange juice. Set aside. Peel and devein shrimp. Cut each nectarine into 6 wedges. Thread the shrimp, nectarines, and onion wedges onto eight long skewers. Grill the shrimp kebabs for 5 minutes, turning once and brushing with BBQ sauce mixture.

Chief Dull Knife Oysters

16 fresh oysters in shells
1 cup lemon juice
6 tablespoons Worcestershire sauce
Hot sauce and garlic salt to taste

Place the fresh whole oysters on the grill, and cook for about 8 minutes, or until they open. Remove the grilled oysters, and slide a knife between the oyster and shell to disconnect. (I always wear heavy gloves when I do this.) Top each oyster with 2 teaspoons lemon juice, 1 teaspoon of Worcestershire sauce, and hot pepper sauce and garlic salt to taste. Serve hot in the shells.

North Carolina Grilled Trout

1/4 cup lemon juice
2 tablespoons melted butter
2 tablespoons olive oil
2 tablespoons chopped parsley
2 tablespoons sesame seeds
1 tablespoon Tabasco sauce
1/2 teaspoon ground ginger
1/2 teaspoon garlic salt
4 trout

In a shallow glass dish, combine the lemon juice, butter, olive oil, parsley, sesame seeds, Tabasco sauce, ginger, and garlic salt; mix well. Pierce the skin of each fish in several places with tines from a fork. Roll the fish in juice mixture to coat the inside and outside of each fish. Cover the dish, and refrigerate for 60 minutes, turning the fish every 10 minutes. Remove the trout from marinade; reserve marinade. Grill the fish for about 10 minutes, turning once and brushing with reserved marinade. The fish is done when it flakes easily with a fork.

Uncle Ronnie Black's Grilled Trout

2 tablespoons olive oil
1 tablespoon lemon juice
1 teaspoon tarragon
$^1/_4$ teaspoon salt
$^1/_4$ teaspoon white pepper
4 large trout fillets

Place the olive oil, lemon juice, tarragon, salt, and white pepper in a large plastic bag. Add the fillets. Close bag, and turn to coat the fish. Refrigerate for 3 hours, turning every hour. Grill the fish for about 8 minutes, turning once. The fish will be finished cooking when it flakes easily with a fork.

Kelly's Grilled Cobia

3 pounds cobia fillets
$^1/_3$ cup olive oil
$^1/_3$ cup lemon juice
2 teaspoons dry mustard
1 minced garlic clove
1 teaspoon salt
$^1/_4$ teaspoon white pepper

Cut the fillets into serving-sized pieces, and place them in a glass bowl. Combine the olive oil and lemon juice. Add all remaining spices to the oil and lemon juice mixture, and mix well with a fork for 1 minute. Pour over the fillets. Marinate for 15 minutes. Grill the cobia fillets for about 8 minutes, turning once and basting with marinade.

Stanfield's Grilled Bass

2 largemouth bass fillets
1 tablespoon melted butter
4 thin red onion slices
4 thin slices of lemon
2 tablespoons sliced almonds
$^1/_4$ cup sliced green onions
$^1/_4$ teaspoon garlic salt
$^1/_4$ teaspoon white pepper

Grease the center of a large sheet of heavy-duty aluminum foil with melted butter. Arrange 2 slices each of the red onion and lemon. Sprinkle with 1 tablespoon almonds and half of the green onions. Arrange the fillets in a single layer over the onions, lemon, and almonds. Top with the remaining red onions, green onions, lemons, and almonds. Sprinkle with garlic salt and white pepper. Wrap fish with foil to seal tight. Grill for about 8 minutes, turning once. The fish is finished cooking when the meat flakes easily with a fork. Serve hot.

Ships Ahoy Grilled Octopus

I dressed, 5-pound octopus
$^1/_2$ cup olive oil
$^1/_4$ cup lemon juice
I tablespoon crushed red pepper flakes
I tablespoon chopped oregano
I tablespoon pepper
2 escarole heads
$^1/_2$ cup mint leaves

Place the dressed octopus in cold water with a cork, and bring to a boil. Simmer on low heat for about 45 minutes. Remove and rinse. Cut the meat into 4 pieces. In a bowl, combine the olive oil, lemon juice, red pepper, oregano, and pepper. Marinate the octopus meat for 20 minutes. Grill for 10 minutes, turning the meat once.

Clean the escarole of the outer leaves. Cut in half lengthwise, and rinse with cold water to remove any grit. Place cut side down on the grill, and cook until lightly charred on both sides. Remove the octopus, and pour remaining marinade over the grilled escarole and octopus slices. Sprinkle with mint and serve hot.

Chicago Grilled Salmon

2 large salmon steaks
$^1/_2$ cup melted butter
$^1/_2$ teaspoon cayenne
$^1/_2$ teaspoon dill
$^1/_2$ cup lemon juice
4 cups brown sugar

Mix together the butter, cayenne, dill, lemon juice, and brown sugar. Grill the salmon steaks for about 10 minutes, turning once and basting with sauce. Serve the steaks with remaining sauce.

Carson's Grilled Crab Legs

12 ounces split crab legs
$1/4$ cup melted butter
1 tablespoon lemon juice
2 teaspoons grated onion
$1/4$ teaspoon tarragon
$1/4$ teaspoon hot pepper sauce

Remove the crab meat from the shells and cut into chunks; return the meat to the shells. Combine the remaining ingredients together and brush over the crab. Place the crab legs, shell side down, on rack about 6 inches above the hot coals. Grill for about 5 minutes, brushing with sauce. Serve hot with remaining sauce.

Singapore Grilled Halibut

6 halibut steaks
$1/2$ cup orange juice
3 tablespoons light soy sauce
2 tablespoons ketchup
2 tablespoons olive oil
2 tablespoons chopped parsley
1 tablespoon lemon juice
$1/2$ teaspoon oregano
$1/2$ teaspoon white pepper
1 minced garlic clove

In a small bowl, combine the orange juice, soy sauce, ketchup, olive oil, parsley, lemon juice, oregano, white pepper, and minced garlic clove. Brush the sauce on the halibut steaks, and refrigerate for 2 hours. Grill the halibut steaks for about 10 minutes, turning once and basting with sauce.

Alex Hartley's BBQ Salmon

I large whole salmon
I tablespoon chopped parsley
³/4 teaspoon dill
¹/2 teaspoon sugar
¹/2 teaspoon salt
I minced garlic clove
¹/2 teaspoon lemon zest
Hickory chips

Mix together the parsley, dill, sugar, salt, garlic, and lemon zest. Rub this mixture on inside and outside of fish. Place the hickory chips on the coals after they have soaked for 60 minutes in water. Grill the salmon with the cover closed for about 10 minutes per side, or until the meat flakes easily with a fork. Serve hot.

CHAPTER NINE

GRILLIN' WITH WILD GAME AND EXOTICS

Grilling with wild game is never boring, though it poses some grilling challenges. When grilling with wild game, you need to realize that you are dealing with the strong flavor of the game itself. I always recommend that it should be prepared boneless, fat trimmed, and any connective tissue removed.

I'm very excited about this chapter. If you're a Cousin Rick Black fan, then you know I love my wild game!

Grilled Gator

4 alligator tail steaks
$^1/_2$ gallon milk
I tablespoon rosemary
I tablespoon red pepper flakes
I teaspoon pepper
$^1/_2$ teaspoon cayenne
I tablespoon olive oil
I cup homemade BBQ sauce

Place the milk in a large glass bowl; add the rosemary and pepper flakes. Season the steaks with pepper and cayenne, and place in milk bowl to cover. Let stand in the cooler for 6 hours. Remove the gator tails from the milk, and pat dry. Season again with pepper and cayenne. Baste the meat with olive oil, and grill for about 30 minutes, turning once. Salt and pepper to taste, and serve with your homemade BBQ sauce.

Turn Water Valley Grilled Gator

4 alligator tail steaks
4 tablespoons melted butter
I teaspoon garlic salt
I tablespoon paprika
I teaspoon cayenne
$^1/_2$ teaspoon black pepper
$^1/_2$ teaspoon white pepper
$^1/_2$ teaspoon thyme
$^1/_2$ teaspoon oregano
$^1/_2$ teaspoon chives
I teaspoon garlic powder

Brush the alligator steaks with melted butter. In a large, shallow dish, combine the garlic salt, paprika, cayenne, black pepper, white pepper, thyme, oregano, chives, and garlic powder. Sprinkle this mixture on all sides of the steaks. Grill for about 30 minutes, turning once.

Weed Patch Grilled Frog Legs

30 small frog legs
I cup beer
6 minced garlic cloves
2 tablespoons honey
$^1/_2$ cup chili sauce
$^1/_4$ teaspoon Louisiana hot sauce
$^1/_4$ teaspoon garlic salt
$^1/_4$ teaspoon white pepper

In a shallow glass dish, combine all the ingredients, and pour over the frog legs. Let sit in the cooler for 4 hours. Grill the frog legs on a covered grill for about 15 minutes, turning once and brushing with sauce.

Ugly Roberts BBQ Turtle Steaks

3 pounds turtle steaks
I cup lime juice
I minced garlic clove
$^1/_4$ cup olive oil
I teaspoon garlic powder with parsley
$^1/_4$ teaspoon pepper
$^1/_4$ teaspoon garlic salt

In a shallow glass dish, soak the turtle steaks in the lime juice and minced garlic for 30 minutes in the cooler. Before grilling, pat the steaks dry. Rub olive oil on all sides of the steaks. Dust both sides of the steaks with garlic powder, pepper, and garlic salt. Grill the steaks for about 30 minutes, turning once.

Lee Tubby's Grilled Rattler

1 large rattlesnake, cleaned and cut into 12-inch pieces
5 tablespoons Dijon mustard
1 teaspoon garlic salt
1 teaspoon Accent
$1/2$ teaspoon black pepper
$1/2$ teaspoon white pepper
$1/2$ teaspoon onion powder
$1/4$ teaspoon celery powder
$1/4$ teaspoon ground coriander
$1/2$ teaspoon cayenne

In a large bowl, combine all the dry spices, and mix together well. Sprinkle the rattlesnake meat with the dry spices to coat the meat. Rub the meat with Dijon mustard, and wrap in plastic. Let the wrapped meat sit for 2 hours in the cooler. Grill the meat over hot coals for about 15 minutes, turning every 5 minutes.

Bardies BBQ Armadillo

4 pounds armadillo meat
$1/2$ cup lemon juice
$1/4$ teaspoon onion salt
$1/4$ teaspoon Accent
$1/4$ teaspoon lemon pepper
$1/2$ pound melted butter
1 cup spicy homemade BBQ sauce

Season the armadillo meat with the lemon juice, onion salt, Accent, and lemon pepper. Rub the seasoned meat with butter. Wrap the meat in heavy aluminum foil and grill for about 45 minutes. Let the meat rest in the foil for 10 minutes before slicing to serve. Serve with BBQ sauce.

Toots Tavern Grilled Rabbit

I large rabbit, cut into serving pieces
2 cups olive oil
7 minced garlic cloves
I cup dry red wine
I teaspoon white pepper
I chopped shallot
6 pitted prunes, chopped
2 cups chicken broth
4 tablespoons balsamic vinegar
$^1/_2$ cup cognac
I tablespoon Accent

Place the olive oil and 4 minced garlic cloves in a small bowl. Add the red wine, and whisk well. Add the white pepper, and whisk again. Place the rabbit in a glass dish, and pour mixture over meat to coat well. Cover, and let sit in the cooler for 36 hours, turning several times.

In a saucepan combine the shallots, remaining minced garlic, prunes, chicken broth, balsamic vinegar, cognac, and Accent. Bring sauce to a boil, and then simmer on low heat for 15 minutes. Grill the marinated rabbit for about 12 minutes per side, turning twice. Serve the sauce with the rabbit.

Quick-N-Easy Grilled Rabbit

3 large rabbits, cut into serving pieces
64 ounces chicken stock
2 cups homemade BBQ sauce

In a large pan or bowl, soak the rabbit meat overnight in heavily salted water. Remove the rabbit meat from the salt water, and rinse well with ice-cold water. Fill a large stock pot with the chicken stock, and add the rabbit meat. Boil the rabbit meat, about three-quarters tender. Remove the meat, and dry it with paper towels. Grill the meat with the cover closed until the meat is tender. Baste with homemade BBQ sauce during the last 10 minutes. Salt and pepper to taste, and serve hot.

Uncle Ted's Bow Kill Grilled Rabbit

2 large rabbits, cut into serving pieces
$1/2$ cup olive oil
8 minced garlic cloves
4 sprigs rosemary
Salt and pepper to taste

Place the rabbit meat in a large zip-top bag, add the remaining ingredients, and coat the meat well. Place the bag with meat in the cooler for 24 hours. Season the rabbit meat with salt and pepper, and grill for about 10 minutes per side.

Toadtown BBQ Wild Boar Chops

8 wild boar chops
I cup lemon juice
2 cups olive oil
$1/2$ cup chopped rosemary
2 tablespoons minced garlic
2 teaspoons sea salt
2 teaspoons ground black peppercorns

Salt and pepper the boar chops. Place the seasoned chops in a shallow glass dish. Whisk together the remaining ingredients, and pour over the chops. Cover, and let marinate in the refrigerator for 8 hours, turning every hour to coat well. Grill the chops with the grill lid closed for about 10 minutes, turning once. Let the cooked chops set for 15 minutes before serving.

Danny Boone's Bear on a Stick

3 pounds bear roast meat
$^1/_2$ cup light soy sauce
2 tablespoons honey
$^1/_4$ cup peanut oil
$^1/_4$ cup lemon juice
I teaspoon curry powder
I teaspoon chili powder
I teaspoon Accent
$^1/_2$ teaspoon smoked salt
$^1/_2$ teaspoon white pepper
2 minced garlic cloves
12 pearl onions
I chopped green bell pepper
I chopped red bell pepper

Cut the bear roast into bite-sized cubes. Mix all the remaining ingredients together, and add the bear meat. (Use a large, shallow glass dish with a cover.) Place the bear meat in the cooler for 6 hours. If using wooden skewers, soak them in water for 60 minutes. Thread the bear meat cubes with the onions, and green and red bell peppers onto the skewers. Grill with the lid closed until the meat reaches your preference.

Barley Soda Springs Grilled Mountain Goat

20 pounds mountain goat meat
1 cup smoked salt
2 tablespoons ground black peppercorns
1 tablespoon cumin
1 teaspoon ground hot pepper flakes
1 cup prepared mustard
$2/3$ cup cider vinegar

In a small bowl, mix together the salt, peppers, and cumin and dust the meat generously. Grill the meat for about 2 hours, turning every 30 minutes. In another bowl, combine the remaining ingredients and baste the meat with this sauce during the last 30 minutes of grill time.

Becky's Moist Beaver

1 large beaver, cleaned and skinned, including tail meat
2 pounds rock salt
2 tablespoons cayenne
2 tablespoons garlic powder with parsley
1 tablespoon white pepper

Place the dressed beaver in a 5-gallon bucket with rock salt, and cover with ice water. Let stand overnight, and repeat this process for 3 days. On the fourth day rinse the beaver carcass well with running water. Season the meat with cayenne, garlic powder, and white pepper. Grill until the meat pulls easily from the bone. Turn the meat every 30 minutes with the grill lid closed.

Buffalo Bill Hayman's Grilled Buffalo Steaks

6 large buffalo rib eye steaks
$1/2$ cup butter
6 sweet onions, peeled and cut in halves
I teaspoon white pepper
2 tablespoons brown sugar
I cup pinot noir
$1/2$ cup wine vinegar
3 tablespoons balsamic vinegar
2 tablespoons cassis
4 sprigs rosemary
2 tablespoons virgin olive oil

In a large saucepan, melt the butter and sauté the onion halves until they are brown and tender. Grill the steaks for about 10 minutes, turning once. While the steaks are grilling, add the remaining ingredients to onions, and simmer on low heat. Serve the steaks with onion sauce.

Seneca Grilled Buffalo Steaks

6 large buffalo steaks
2 cups olive oil
4 minced garlic cloves
I cup dry red wine
I tablespoon Accent
I teaspoon ground black pepper

In a large, shallow glass dish, mix together the olive oil, garlic, red wine, Accent, and black pepper. Coat the steaks in marinade for 6 hours in the cooler. Drain the steaks from the marinade, and grill for about 10 minutes, turning once and basting with remaining marinade.

Spring Mountain Grilled Antelope

4 large antelope steaks
1 cup lemon juice
$^1/_2$ cup chopped onion
$^1/_2$ cup olive oil
1 teaspoon Accent
1 teaspoon celery seeds
1 teaspoon thyme
$^1/_4$ teaspoon onion salt
$^1/_4$ teaspoon rosemary
$^1/_4$ teaspoon oregano
3 minced garlic cloves

In a shallow glass bowl, combine all the ingredients except the antelope steaks. Add the steaks, and marinate for 8 hours in the cooler. Grill the steaks for about 20 minutes, turning once and basting often with remaining marinade.

Melee Barbecued Venison Steaks

4 large venison steaks, trimmed of fat
1 pound butter
2 cups beer
$^1/_4$ cup Worcestershire sauce
$^1/_2$ cup lemon juice
3 chopped white onions
2 teaspoons sea salt
1 teaspoon white pepper

In a saucepan, add all the ingredients except the steaks, and simmer for 30 minutes on low heat. Grill the steaks over hot coals for about 20 minutes, turning once. Baste the steaks with BBQ sauce during the last 10 minutes of grill time. Serve the steaks with sauce.

From the Timber to the Table
Venison Chops

12 venison chops, trimmed of fat

1 cup olive oil

$^1/_2$ cup white wine

5 teaspoons Dijon mustard

2 teaspoons minced garlic

1 teaspoon balsamic vinegar

1 teaspoon Accent

Place the venison chops in a large zip-top-style bag. Combine the remaining ingredients, and pour over chops. Seal bag, and let stand in the cooler for 2 hours. Discard the used sauce, and grill the chops over hot coals with the lid closed for about 20 minutes, turning once.

Samuel D. Cochenour's Smoked Leg of Venison

1 whole venison leg, with bottom round

2 gallons water

2 cups quick salt

1 cup light soy sauce

1/2 cup Worcestershire sauce

1/2 cup brown sugar

1/2 cup paprika

4 tablespoons thyme

4 tablespoons oregano

4 tablespoons cumin

2 tablespoons coriander

2 tablespoons ground black peppercorns

2 tablespoons garlic powder with parsley

1 cup olive oil

In a very large bowl or dish, combine the water, salt, soy sauce, Worcestershire sauce, and sugar, stirring until the salt has dissolved. Place the venison leg in the brine. Refrigerate the leg with brine for 48 hours. In a large bowl, combine the remaining ingredients except the olive oil. Remove the venison leg from the brine and dry with a paper towel. Rub the leg to coat with first the olive oil and then the spices from bowl. Prepare the smoker with hickory wood. Smoke on slow setting for about 6 hours. Cool, and slice into thin serving pieces.

Cousin Rick Black's Grilled Venison

10 pounds venison shoulder meat

2 cups cider vinegar

1 cup dark beer

$^1/_2$ cup brown sugar

2 teaspoons red pepper flakes

2 tablespoons Louisiana hot sauce

Garlic salt and pepper to taste

2 cups olive oil

1 tablespoon garlic salt

1 tablespoon lemon pepper

In a saucepan, combine the vinegar, beer, brown sugar, pepper flakes, hot sauce, and garlic salt and pepper to taste. Simmer sauce for 30 minutes, stirring often. Rub the venison shoulder meat with olive oil, garlic salt, and lemon pepper. Grill on medium heat for about 2 hours, basting with sauce.

Iowa Grilled Venison

1 large venison roast, trimmed of fat

4 crushed garlic cloves

12 ounces beef consommé

2 cups dark beer

1 tablespoon garlic powder with parsley

1 tablespoon apple cider

1 tablespoon onion salt

6 slices of thick-cut smoked bacon

Marinate the roast overnight in a sealed glass dish with the garlic, beef consommé, beer, garlic powder with parsley, cider, and onion salt. When ready for grilling, place the bacon strips on top of roast, and seal all in a heavy foil. Grill for about 2 hours, turning every 30 minutes. Let the roast sit in the foil for 20 minutes before slicing to serve.

Chickasawhatchee Grilled Venison

5 venison tenderloin steaks
2 cups olive oil
2 cups honey
2 cups 7Up soda
$^1/_2$ cup white vinegar
40 ounces crushed pineapple, undrained
$^1/_2$ cup prepared mustard
$^1/_2$ cup Worcestershire sauce
1 teaspoon Accent
1 teaspoon garlic salt

Combine all the sauce ingredients in a shallow glass dish, and pour over venison tenderloins. Place the venison and sauce in the cooler for 12 hours. Discard the sauce, and grill the venison over medium coals for about 30 minutes, turning every 10 minutes. Let the meat rest for 5 minutes before serving.

Okahumpka Grilled Duck Breast Fillets

4 duck breast fillets
4 bacon slices
2 beef bouillon cubes
I cup water
I tablespoon red current jelly
$^1/_2$ teaspoon dry mustard
2 tablespoons sherry
I tablespoon brandy
$^1/_4$ teaspoon marjoram
$^1/_4$ teaspoon oregano
$^1/_2$ teaspoon Accent
I tablespoon orange zest

Wrap each duck breast fillet with a slice of bacon and season with salt and pepper. Grill over hot coals for about 3 minutes per side. Dissolve the beef bouillon cubes in 1 cup water in a large cast iron skillet. Stir in the jelly, mustard, sherry, brandy, and remaining spices, simmering until sauce thickens. Stir in the orange zest, and add the grilled duck fillets. Simmer in sauce for about 8 minutes, basting all sides of duck with sauce. Serve hot with sauce.

Sopchoppy Grilled Wood Duck

5 wood ducks
¹/₄ cup olive oil
3 tablespoons lemon juice
2 teaspoons dried thyme
I teaspoon Accent
I teaspoon ground pepper
I cup dried cherries
3 tablespoons brandy
³/₄ cup orange juice
2 cups dry red wine
¹/₃ cup balsamic vinegar
2 cups chicken broth
Zest of one orange

Combine the olive oil, lemon juice, thyme, Accent, and pepper in a small bowl, and whisk together. Set this mixture aside. Split the ducks up the back, and lay flat. Place the ducks in a glass container, and pour marinade over all. Soak the cherries in the brandy and orange juice in a small bowl for about 30 minutes. Add the cherries with juice along with remaining ingredients to a saucepan, and simmer for 30 minutes. Grill the ducks over hot coals for about 10 minutes, turning once and basting with sauce from saucepan.

Old Mother Hubbard's Grilled Goose Kebabs

4 goose breasts, boneless and skinless
16 ounces Italian salad oil
1 tablespoon garlic salt
4 large sweet yellow onions
4 green bell peppers
1 pound thick-cut smoked bacon

Cut the goose breasts into 1-inch cubes. Marinate them in the Italian oil with garlic salt for 48 hours in the cooler, stirring 4 times daily. Quarter onions, and separate into layers. Cut the bell peppers into 1-inch squares. Cut the bacon into serving-sized pieces. On a well-soaked skewer, place the bacon on each side of goose meat cubes. Alternate the onions and peppers with each piece of goose meat. Continue on skewers until all the ingredients are used. Grill for about 20 minutes, turning and basting with remaining marinade every 5 minutes.

Chaser Ranch Grilled Quail

4 quail
$1/2$ cup olive oil
1 teaspoon onion salt
1 teaspoon lemon pepper
2 pints ketchup
1 cup cooking sherry
$1/2$ cup corn syrup
3 teaspoons Louisiana hot sauce
3 tablespoons chili powder
2 tablespoons Worcestershire sauce
1 tablespoon Accent

Split the quail, and season all sides with the olive oil, onion salt, and lemon pepper. Begin cooking on grill. Meanwhile, combine the ketchup, sherry, corn syrup, hot sauce, chili powder, Worcestershire sauce, and Accent. Start basting the quail with this sauce after 15 minutes of grill time. The quail is finished when the meat is tender to the fork and the sauce is slightly charred.

Odessa Grilled Quail

10 dressed quail
1 cup melted butter
1 teaspoon garlic powder with parsley
$1/2$ teaspoon salt
10 thick-cut bacon slices
1 cup home BBQ sauce

Combine the butter, garlic powder with parsley, and salt; brush on all sides of the quail. Wrap 1 slice of bacon around each quail, and secure with wooden picks. Grill the quail for about 45 minutes, turning twice. Remove picks and serve with homemade BBQ sauce.

Cousin Rick Black's Dove Hunter's Grill

12 dressed and cleaned doves

1 pound thick-cut bacon

12 ounces Worcestershire sauce

5 minced garlic cloves

5 tablespoons chili powder

1 tablespoon salt

3 tablespoons freshly ground black peppercorns

10 ounces Dijon mustard

1 pound butter

3 quartered lemons

2 quartered limes

3 tablespoons Accent

4 tablespoons Louisiana hot sauce

Wrap the whole doves in strips of bacon, and anchor with wooden picks. Place the wrapped doves in a flat glass pan, and baste with the remaining ingredients that have been combined in a mixing bowl. Let the doves sit for 60 minutes in a cooler. Grill until the bacon is crisp, and the dove meat is tender, basting with sauce while cooking.

CHAPTER TEN

GRILLIN' WITH FRUITS AND VEGGIES

I can't really think of any fruit that cannot be cooked on the grill. Even hard fruits such as pears, pineapples, and apples are as easy to grill as their softer cousins peaches, plums, and papaya.

And when it comes to grillin' veggies, well I'm here to tell you that ain't no better way to cook a tatter or onions than on your grill! The flavor of veggies is always intensified when seasoned, buttered, and grilled.

Larry Humphrey's Fort Madison Iowa Grilled Plums

12 plums, cut in halves
$^1/_2$ cup melted butter
$^1/_4$ cup Jack Daniels
2 cups brown sugar
$^1/_2$ cup lemon juice
$^1/_4$ cup lime juice
$^1/_2$ cup water

Place the Jack Daniels in a medium saucepan, and bring it to a boil. Add the butter, brown sugar, lemon juice, lime juice, and water. Stir with a whisk until all the sugar is dissolved. Let sauce simmer on low heat for about 3 minutes. Brush the plum halves with the sauce, and grill for about 5 minutes, turning once and basting with sauce. Serve with remaining sauce.

Grilled Havana

5 ounces cream cheese, softened
1 tablespoon honey
1 sliced red pear
1 sliced red apple
$^1/_2$ sliced cantaloupe
2 sliced bananas
$^1/_2$ cup melted butter
2 tablespoons soft honey
1 tablespoon cinnamon

In a small glass bowl, combine the cream cheese and 1 tablespoon honey. In another glass bowl, combine the butter and the other tablespoon honey. Baste the fruit slices with the butter and honey sauce, and grill the slices for about 2 minutes, turning once. Serve the grilled fruit with the cream cheese and honey mixture. Dust the tops of fruit with cinnamon.

PA-PA-PA Pineapples on the Q

1 pineapple, peeled, cored, cut into $1/2$-inch slices
$1/2$ cup brown sugar
1 tablespoon lime juice
1 tablespoon lemon juice
$1/2$ teaspoon cinnamon

In a small bowl, combine the brown sugar, lime juice, lemon juice, and cinnamon. Brush this mixture on the pineapple slices, and grill for about 10 minutes, or until the fruit is tender. Serve hot.

Krissy's Grilled Strawberries

16 large strawberries
2 tablespoons balsamic vinegar
2 tablespoons white sugar

Coat each strawberry with the balsamic vinegar, and then roll them in the sugar. Grill them for 2 minutes, turning once.

Grilled Fruit with a Buzz

4 sliced nectarines
8 sliced plums
2 cups blueberries
$1/2$ cup Cointreau liqueur
1 tablespoon white sugar

Make a foil boat with heavy foil. Spray the insides of the foil boat with cooking spray. Place the fruit inside the foil boat, and drizzle with the Cointreau liqueur. Seal the boats, and grill for about 20 minutes, turning once. Sprinkle the grilled fruit with sugar, and serve.

Muscatine Grilled Cantaloupe

1 cantaloupe, peeled, seeded, and cubed
$1/4$ cup butter
$1/2$ cup honey
$1/2$ teaspoon balsamic vinegar
$1/3$ cup chopped mint leaves

In a small saucepan, heat the butter, honey, and balsamic vinegar. Stir in the chopped mint, and simmer for 2 minutes. Thread the cantaloupe cubes onto skewers, and baste with mint sauce. Make sure the grill is lightly coated with oil so the fruit does not stick. Grill for about 8 minutes, turning every 2 minutes.

Pineapple-A-Brandy Go Go

8 slices pineapple
3 tablespoons honey
5 tablespoons peach brandy
2 teaspoons lime juice

Combine the honey, brandy, and lime juice in a glass dish. Add the pineapple slices, cover, and let sit in the refrigerator for 2 hours, turning every 30 minutes. Grill the pineapple slices for about 10 minutes, turning every 2 minutes. Serve when the pineapple is starting to caramelize.

Jamakinmebannanuts!

3 bananas, cut crosswise in half
$^1/_3$ cup soft honey
$^1/_4$ cup pineapple juice
$^1/_4$ cup finely chopped macadamia nuts

Thread one banana half lengthwise onto a skewer. In a glass bowl combine the honey and pineapple juice. Dip and brush each skewered banana in honey sauce, and grill for about 3 minutes, turning once while basting with honey sauce. Lightly roll the grilled bananas in nuts before serving.

Brenda's Peaches

6 peaches, halved and pitted
1 tablespoon butter
2 tablespoons brown sugar
$^1/_4$ cup dark rum

In a saucepan, melt the butter. Remove from heat, and add the brown sugar and rum. Stir until the sugar is dissolved. Place the peach halves in a glass dish, and add the rum sauce, stirring to coat the fruit well. Let the peaches sit for 15 minutes after stirring. Grill the peaches, cut side up, until you can see the grill marks on the sides. Turn the peaches over, and do the same. Serve the grilled peaches topped with any remaining sauce.

Old Dale Mizer's Grilled Sweet Pineapple

I sliced pineapple
$^1/_2$ cup melted butter
I cup white sugar
I teaspoon cinnamon
$^1/_4$ teaspoon ground cloves
I teaspoon lime zest

In a bowl, combine the sugar, cinnamon, cloves, and lime zest. Dip the pineapple slices in the melted butter and then into the sugar mixture. Grill for about 5 minutes, turning the fruit every minute, until golden brown.

Cousin Larry "Chopper's" Daddy's Home Pineapple

I pineapple, sliced
$^1/_2$ cup melted butter
$^3/_4$ cup white sugar
$^1/_4$ cup cheap whiskey
I tablespoon cinnamon
I tablespoon lime juice
$^1/_4$ teaspoon ground cloves
I teaspoon lime zest

In a glass dish, combine the sugar, whiskey, cinnamon, lime juice, cloves, and zest. Dip pineapple slices first in the melted butter and then into the sauce. Grill the pineapples for about 8 minutes, turning every minute, and basting with sauce.

Scotty Vaughan's Missouri-Style Grilled Cantaloupe

I cantaloupe, peeled and cubed
$1/4$ cup butter
$1/4$ cup red wine
$1/2$ cup honey
$1/3$ cup chopped mint leaves
I tablespoon cinnamon

Thread the cantaloupe cubes onto skewers. In a saucepan, heat the butter with the red wine, honey, mint, and cinnamon; stir for 3 minutes on low simmer. Brush the cantaloupe skewers with sauce several times until they are coated well. Grill for about 6 minutes, turning once and basting with any remaining sauce.

Jerry Anderson's "I'm Single So I Don't Care" Grilled Pineapples

I fresh sliced pineapple
I tablespoon sugar
I tablespoon rum
I teaspoon cinnamon

Place the pineapple slices in a glass dish along with the sugar, rum, and cinnamon. Let the mixture sit in the fridge, covered, for 8 hours. Grill for about 3 minutes per side, and serve hot.

Daddy Fast Grilled Apples

4 large baking apples
2 tablespoons cinnamon
2 tablespoons sugar

Wash, dry, and core apples. In a small bowl, combine the cinnamon and sugar. Place each apple on the center of an aluminum foil sheet; spoon the cinnamon and sugar mixture into the apple cores, wrap tight with the foil, and grill for about 10 minutes, or until the apples are tender. Serve hot.

Casey's Grilled Apple Rings

$1/3$ cup sugar
$1/2$ teaspoon cinnamon
$1/2$ cup melted butter
5 baking apples, cored and cut crosswise into 1-inch slices.

Mix the sugar and cinnamon together in a small bowl, and set aside. Brush all sides of the apple slices with melted butter. Sprinkle the slices with the sugar mixture, and grill for about 10 minutes, turning once.

Holland Veggies by Mike Hoffman

2 medium potatoes
¹/₂ pound baby carrots
1 green bell pepper
1 medium onion (optional)
3 tablespoons margarine
1 tablespoon Mrs. Dash

Slice skinned potatoes into small wedges. Take an 18-inch-long piece of tin foil, and lay potatoes wedges side by side. Cut green peppers into rings, and then have them. Insert baby carrots between potato wedges. Spread green peppers evenly on top of the potatoes and carrots. If using onion, slice and spread it evenly on top of green peppers. Distribute 3 tablespoons margarine evenly on top, and sprinkle with Mrs. Dash. Wrap in foil, and wrap again with a second 18-inch piece of foil. Cook on Holland grill for about 45 minutes. Cooking time will vary on other grills.

"I Think I'm Turning Japanese" Grilled Eggplant

6 Japanese eggplants
3 tablespoons olive oil
1 teaspoon minced garlic
¹/₂ teaspoon garlic salt
¹/₂ teaspoon white pepper

Lightly coat the eggplants with olive oil, garlic, garlic salt, and white pepper. Place the seasoned eggplants on the grill, and grill for about 8 minutes, turning every 2 minutes.

B-Rad Hyden's "Keepin' It Real Skillet" Grilled 2-maytoes

6 large tomatoes
I green pepper
$^1/_2$ cup white sugar
I cup seasoned dried breadcrumbs
Butter for dotting
I tablespoon garlic salt with parsley

Cut the tomatoes in half. Remove all stems. Slice the green pepper into rings. Place the green peppers and tomatoes into a large boat of heavy foil. Sprinkle with sugar and breadcrumbs. Add a dot of butter in the center of each veggie. Dust the tops of all with garlic salt with parsley. Seal tightly with foil, and grill for about 20 minutes, turning every 2 minutes until the veggies are tender and done.

Calfie's Grilled Corn

6 ears of corn with husks on
I stick of butter
Salt and pepper to taste

Pull back a small amount of corn husk. Put small amount of butter on corn. Put the husks back over again. Wrap the corn in heavy foil. Grill for about 30 minutes. Salt and pepper to taste.

Sonoma Grilled Corn

8 ears of cleaned corn
1/2 cup softened butter
2 tablespoons parsley
2 tablespoons chives
1/2 teaspoon salt
1/4 teaspoon white pepper

In a small bowl, mix together the butter, parsley, chives, salt, and white pepper. Spread a tablespoon of butter mixture on each ear of corn; wrap each ear individually in heavy foil. Grill for about 25 minutes, turning every 5 minutes.

Grilled Cabbage

1 head of cabbage
1/4 cup butter
1 yellow onion
6 slices of thick-cut bacon
1/2 teaspoon garlic salt
1/4 teaspoon pepper

Chop and dice all the ingredients, and wrap all in heavy foil. Grill with the lid closed for about 45 minutes, turning the foil wrap twice. Serve hot.

Grilled Taters

8 potatoes
1 red onion
8 slices of American cheese
Salt and pepper to taste

Slice the potatoes into thin slices. Slice the onion into rings. Layer the potatoes and onions in the center of a large strip of foil. Place the cheese slices on top to cover all. Salt and pepper and seal foil. Grill for about 45 minutes, turning foil packet twice.

Yankee Grilled Tomatoes

6 firm red tomatoes
1/4 cup melted butter
1/3 cup breadcrumbs
1/4 cup minced basil
Garlic salt and white pepper to taste

Cut the tomatoes in half, and place them in a well-oiled grilling basket. Brush each tomato half with melted butter, and sprinkle with breadcrumbs, minced basil, garlic salt, and white pepper. Grill with the lid closed for about 8 minutes, or until the tomatoes turn brown and bubbly.

Tator's Grilled Sweet Potatoes

I pound sweet potatoes, peeled and sliced
2 tablespoons soy sauce
2 tablespoons soft honey
2 tablespoons light beer
I minced garlic clove
I tablespoon olive oil

Wrap the sweet potatoes in plastic wrap. Cook in the microwave on high for 3 minutes. Combine the soy sauce, honey, beer, and garlic in a large bowl. Add the sweet potatoes, and gently toss them to coat well. Drain, keeping the marinade. Arrange in a single layer in an oiled grilling basket. Brush the potatoes slices with the olive oil. Grill for about 20 minutes, basting with marinade.

Grilled Asparagus

I pound asparagus
4 tablespoons lemon juice
$^1/_4$ cup olive oil
2 minced garlic cloves
2 teaspoons dill weed
Garlic salt and pepper to taste

Remove the bottom third of the asparagus, and place spears in a large glass dish. Add the remaining ingredients, and marinate for 2 hours, turning every 30 minutes. Place skewers through the middle of the asparagus. Grill until the asparagus becomes brown and crunchy.

Grilled Potatoes

5 sliced potatoes
I sliced red onion
I teaspoon salt
I teaspoon pepper
5 tablespoons butter
I package of real bacon bits

Measure out 3 sheets of aluminum foil large enough to easily wrap over all the veggies, and layer foil one on top of the other. Place the potatoes and onion in the center, sprinkle with salt and pepper, and dot with butter. Sprinkle on the bacon bits. Wrap into a flattened square, and seal the edges. Grill the foil package for about 30 minutes, turning twice.

BBQ Potatoes

I2 small potatoes, peeled and halved
$^1/_2$ cup vegetable oil
2 tablespoons seasoned salt
I tablespoon garlic powder

Place the potatoes in a large pan with enough lightly salted water to cover. Bring the potatoes to a boil, and then simmer on low heat for 20 minutes. Drain the potatoes, and pat dry. Coat the potatoes thoroughly with the vegetable oil, seasoned salt, and garlic powder. Grill them for about 15 minutes, turning once.

Grilled BBQ Veggies

$1/2$ cup sliced zucchini
$1/2$ cup sliced red bell pepper
$1/2$ cup sliced yellow bell pepper
$1/2$ cup sliced yellow squash
$1/2$ cup sliced red onion
18 large button mushrooms
18 cherry tomatoes
$1/2$ cup olive oil
$1/2$ cup soy sauce
$1/2$ cup lemon juice
1 crushed garlic clove
1 teaspoon sea salt
1 teaspoon black pepper

Place all the ingredients together in a large glass dish, and toss well to coat. Cover the dish, and let marinate in the refrigerator for 1 hour. Remove the veggies from the marinade, and grill for about 20 minutes, turning once.

Oink Grilled Vegetables

1 thick-sliced eggplant
2 red bell peppers, halved and seeded
2 yellow bell peppers, halved and seeded
2 thick-sliced zucchinis
2 thick-sliced red onions
12 cherry tomatoes
5 tablespoons olive oil
1 cup teriyaki sauce

Brush all the veggies with olive oil to coat. Brush the grill grate with oil, and grill the veggies for about 20 minutes, turning twice and brushing with teriyaki sauce. Salt and pepper to taste, and serve hot.

CHAPTER ELEVEN

MY FAVORITE GRILLIN' SIDES

This chapter covers my favorite grillin' side dishes: potato salads, baked beans, and cole slaws. My mouth be talkin' to my lips, sayin', "Get old Cousin Rick on the stick!" Let's get on with this fun chapter. Make sure you try every recipe in this chapter; you'll be glad you did!

Raisin Slaw

1 cup unpeeled, cored, and diced red apples
$^1/_2$ cup raisins
$^1/_2$ cup mayo
3 cups shredded cabbage
1 teaspoon Accent

Combine the diced apples, raisins, mayo, and Accent. Chill for 2 hours. Add the cabbage and serve.

Tasty Coleslaw

2 pounds shredded cabbage
1 cup sugar
1 cup white wine
1 teaspoon garlic salt with parsley
1 cup whipping cream
1 teaspoon white pepper

Place the cabbage in a large glass bowl, cover, and chill for one hour. Add the sugar, wine, garlic salt, whipping cream, and white pepper to chilled cabbage, and toss well. Cover, and chill for another hour; serve.

Slangy Tangy Slaw

I pound shredded cabbage
I diced red onion
I shredded carrot
I cup sugar
I teaspoon salt
I teaspoon dry mustard
I teaspoon celery seed
I cup vinegar
$2/3$ cup vegetable oil

Combine the shredded cabbage with the diced onion and carrot, and chill for 1 hour. Meanwhile, add the remaining ingredients to a saucepan, and bring to a boil. Pour this sauce over the cabbage mixture, and chill for another 2 hours. Toss well and serve.

Slaw of the South

I pound shredded cabbage
I chopped bell pepper
I chopped white onion
3 grated carrots
I cup sugar
I teaspoon salt
$2/3$ cup vegetable oil
I teaspoon dry mustard
I teaspoon celery seed
I cup cider vinegar

In a large glass bowl, combine the cabbage, peppers, onion, and carrots. Chill for 1 hour. In a saucepan, add the remaining ingredients, and bring to a boil. Simmer for 15 minutes. Pour hot mixture over cabbage mixture, and toss well. Chill all for another 30 minutes, and serve.

Adam Zapel's Creamy Slaw

1 pound shredded cabbage
1 teaspoon dry mustard
1 teaspoon salt
1 teaspoon sugar
1 teaspoon flour
2 eggs, beaten
3/4 cup milk
2 tablespoons cider vinegar
2 tablespoons lime juice
1 tablespoon butter

Place the cabbage in a bowl, and let stand in a cooler for 60 minutes. Add the remaining ingredients to a saucepan, and simmer for 15 minutes. Add the sauce to the cabbage and mix well. Chill all for 1 hour and then serve.

Old-Time Coleslaw

1 pound shredded cabbage
1/2 cup white sugar
1/3 cup white vinegar
1 teaspoon salt
1 cup whipping cream
1/4 cup diced bacon, precooked

Place the cabbage in a large glass bowl, and chill for 2 hours. Blend the remaining ingredients together. Add to the cabbage, and toss. Serve ice cold.

Slaw BBQ Side

1 pound shredded cabbage
3 carrots, shredded
1 finely chopped green bell pepper
2 cups mayonnaise
3 tablespoons white sugar
1 tablespoon vinegar
$1/4$ cup chopped chives
$1/4$ cup minced green onions

In a large glass dish or bowl, combine all the ingredients, and toss well for 2 minutes. Chill for 1 hour, and then toss again for 1 minute; serve.

Yep Em Slaw

1 pound shredded cabbage
2 teaspoons smoked oysters
1 minced onion
1 cup vinegar
1 teaspoon salt
1 teaspoon celery seed
1 teaspoon dry mustard
$3/4$ cup olive oil

In a large glass bowl, add together the cabbage, oysters, and onion. Chill for 1 hour, covered. Combine the remaining ingredients, and simmer for 5 minutes. Pour the hot mixture over the cabbage, and toss well. Let all chill for 60 minutes, and then serve.

Hot Tater Salad

6 potatoes
6 slices smoked bacon
$^1/_2$ cup chopped onions
$^1/_4$ cup chopped green bell pepper
$^1/_4$ cup vinegar
$^1/_4$ cup water
I teaspoon salt
$^1/_2$ teaspoon white pepper

Peel the potatoes, and then place them in a large pot covered with lightly salted water. Cook them until they are tender; slice into thin pieces. In a large skillet, fry the bacon, onions, and green bell pepper until brown; add the vinegar, water, salt, and white pepper. Add potatoes; cover and simmer for 15 minutes. Serve hot.

Potato Salad Recipe

4 cups diced cooked red potatoes
$^3/_4$ cup chopped celery
2 tablespoons minced red bell pepper
I tablespoon diced pimento
2 tablespoons chopped sweet pickles
$^1/_2$ cup mayonnaise
I teaspoon Accent
$^1/_2$ teaspoon black pepper
I teaspoon prepared mustard
2 teaspoon lemon juice
$^1/_2$ cup heavy cream

In a large glass bowl, combine all the ingredients, and mix well. Chill the salad for 1 hour before serving.

Iowa Potato Salad

I pound small red potatoes, cooked and drained
I cup mayonnaise
$^1/_3$ cup sour cream
$^1/_4$ cup milk
3 tablespoons spicy mustard
$^1/_2$ teaspoon garlic salt
$^1/_4$ cup cooked sweet corn, drained
$^1/_4$ cup chopped red onion
$^1/_4$ cup chopped ham
$^1/_4$ cup chopped celery
$^1/_4$ cup chopped red bell pepper

Cube the cooked potatoes, and chill them for 1 hour in a large glass bowl. In another bowl, combine the remaining ingredients, and mix well. Add this mixture to the chilled potatoes, and mix all using a fork. Salt and pepper to taste, and serve.

Favorite Potato Salad

6 cups cooked and diced red potatoes
$^1/_2$ cup diced cucumber
$^1/_4$ cup chopped celery
2 tablespoons minced white onion
I teaspoon seasoned salt
I teaspoon white pepper
I cup sour cream
$^1/_2$ cup mayonnaise
$^1/_4$ cup cider vinegar
2 teaspoons mustard
4 hard-boiled eggs, chopped

Combine all the ingredients in a large bowl, and mix well. Chill the salad for 1 hour before serving. Salt or pepper to taste, and serve.

Warm Potato Salad

8 slices thick-cut bacon
2 tablespoons flour
1 tablespoon white sugar
1 teaspoon seasoned salt
1 teaspoon black pepper
1 tablespoon prepared mustard
$^{1}/_{2}$ cup vinegar
1 cup water
5 cups cooked potatoes, cubed

Cook the bacon in a large skillet; set aside. Heat the drippings; blend in the flour, sugar, seasoned salt, pepper, and mustard. Mix well until smooth. Add the remaining ingredients, and stir. Simmer for 5 minutes on low heat, and serve.

Soft Potato Salad

6 cups hot mashed potatoes
$^{1}/_{2}$ cup diced celery
$^{1}/_{4}$ cup diced red bell pepper
1 cup mayonnaise
$^{1}/_{2}$ cup chopped yellow onion
$^{1}/_{4}$ cup milk
$^{1}/_{4}$ cup vinegar
1 tablespoon dry mustard
1 teaspoon garlic salt
1 teaspoon black pepper

In a large bowl, combine the hot mashed potatoes with the remaining ingredients, and mix well. Add more salt and pepper if desired. Serve.

Maine-Style Potato Salad

$1/2$ pound crabmeat
I pound potatoes
I cup mayonnaise
3 tablespoons sour cream
$1/4$ cup lemon juice
3 scallions, minced
I tablespoon parsley
I teaspoon garlic salt
$1/2$ teaspoon white pepper

Chop the crabmeat into small pieces, and set them in the cooler. Peel the potatoes, and place them in a pot covered in lightly salted water. Cook the potatoes until they are tender. Let the potatoes cool, and then cut them into small cubes. Add the remaining ingredients to the potatoes. Stir, and add the crabmeat. Stir all again, and serve.

Wild Side Potato Salad

4 pounds potatoes
I chopped white onion
$1/2$ cup chopped green onions
$1/4$ cup chopped dill pickle
2 cups mayo
I pound imitation crabmeat, chopped
I teaspoon Accent

Peel and boil the potatoes. Drain when tender; cool. Dice the potatoes, and add the remaining ingredients. Check for seasoning. Chill for 1 hour before serving.

Bean and Tater Salad

I pound cooked and cleaned green beans
I pound cooked and cubed potatoes
I cup minced sweet onion
$^1/_2$ cup chopped green bell peppers
$^1/_4$ cup vegetable oil
$^1/_4$ cup garlic wine vinegar
$^1/_4$ cup rice vinegar
I teaspoon garlic salt with parsley
I teaspoon sugar

In a large bowl, combine the cooked green beans and potato cubes. Toss together using your hands. In another bowl combine the remaining ingredients, and stir well. Add this mixture to the green beans and potatoes, and stir well. Chill the salad for 2 hours before serving.

Picnic Salad

3 pounds red potatoes
$^1/_2$ cup chopped onion
$^1/_2$ cup chopped celery
$^1/_4$ cup chopped dill pickle
2 tablespoons parsley
$^1/_4$ cup bacon bits
I teaspoon seasoned salt
I teaspoon white pepper
3 tablespoons balsamic vinegar
2 tablespoons vegetable oil
I cup mayonnaise

Peel and cube the potatoes. Cook the potatoes until they are tender. Drain water from pot, and allow the potatoes to cool. In a large mixing bowl, combine the remaining ingredients, and stir well. Add the cooked potatoes to mixture, and stir again. Add more seasoning if desired, and serve.

Bubba's BBQ Baked Beans

2 16-ounce cans of pork and beans, drained
1 cup spicy homemade **BBQ** sauce
$^1/_2$ cup brown sugar
1 chopped apple
$^1/_2$ cup minced white onions
2 tablespoons raisins
1 teaspoon prepared mustard
6 strips thick-cut bacon
Salt and pepper to taste

Place all the ingredients together in a large baking dish, topping mixture with the bacon slices. Bake for about an hour at 350 degrees.

Billy Wilke's Deer Camp Beans

1 pound ground venison
1 pound chopped bacon
1 cup chopped onions
$^1/_2$ cup ketchup
$^1/_2$ cup homemade **BBQ** sauce
1 teaspoon garlic salt
1 teaspoon pepper
$^1/_2$ teaspoon hot sauce
5 tablespoons mustard
5 tablespoons molasses
1 tablespoon chili powder
3 16-ounce cans of pork and beans, drained
3 16-ounce cans of kidney beans, drained

Brown the venison, bacon, and onion. Drain the fat. In a large baking dish, combine cooked venison mixture with the remaining ingredients. Bake for about 65 minutes at 350 degrees.

Dean Fields's BBQ Bean Dish

2 pounds hamburger

1 cup chopped white onion

2 16-ounce cans of pork and beans, drained

1 cup homemade BBQ sauce

1 tablespoon chili powder

1 cup cheddar cheese

6 frozen buttermilk biscuits

In a large skillet, brown the hamburger and onions. Drain off any fat, and add the beans, BBQ sauce, chili powder, and cheese. Pour this mixture into a large baking dish. Cut the buttermilk biscuits in half, and place them with the cut side down on top of bean mixture. Bake for about 20 minutes at 350 degrees, and serve hot.

West Point Sweet Corn Festival Beans

1 pound ground pork

6 strips thick-cut smoked bacon, chopped

1 cup chopped yellow onion

1 cup Cousin Rick Black's BBQ sauce

1 teaspoon salt

4 tablespoons prepared mustard

5 tablespoons molasses

1 teaspoon chili powder

1 teaspoon hot sauce

1 teaspoon pepper

3 16-ounce cans of pork and beans, drained

3 16-ounce cans of red kidney beans

1 16-ounce can of sweet corn, drained

Brown the ground pork, chopped bacon, and onion. Drain the excess fat. Add the remaining ingredients, stirring while adding each. Place the mixture in a large baking dish, and bake for 60 minutes at 350 degrees.

Travis's U of I Slow Cooker Beans

1 pound bacon
1/2 cup chopped onions
1/2 cup chopped green bell pepper
1/2 teaspoon minced garlic
1/4 cup chopped celery
6 cups pork and beans, drained
1 cup dad's BBQ sauce
1/2 cup white syrup
1 teaspoon salt
1 teaspoon white pepper

In a skillet, fry the bacon until crisp. Remove from pan and break into bits. Cook the onions, green peppers, and garlic in bacon fat. Add all the remaining ingredients including the bacon to skillet, and simmer for 5 minutes. Place the mixture in a large slow cooker, and cook on low until ready to serve.

Swamp Turner's Hot Lips Beans

2 pounds hamburger
1 pound sausage
1 cup minced red onion
1 cup chopped green bell pepper
1 gallon pork and beans, drained
2 cups homemade BBQ sauce
1 tablespoon cayenne
1 cup brown sugar
1/2 cup mustard
1 tablespoon garlic salt
1 tablespoon white pepper
1/2 cup ketchup
2 tablespoons hot sauce

In a large skillet, brown the hamburger and sausage, add the onion and green bell pepper, and cook until the veggies are tender. Place all ingredients in a kettle, and simmer on low until ready to serve. Check for seasonings.

ABBREVIATIONS

So, how did *Grillin' Like a Villain* measure up? Use my measurement calculator to find out!

Gallon: gal.
Ounce: oz.
Pint: pt.
Quart: qt.
Tablespoon: Tbls.
Teaspoon: tsp.

1 tsp.	=	$^1/_3$ Tbls. or $^1/_{64}$ cup or $^1/_6$ oz.
2 tsp.	=	$^2/_3$ Tbls. or $^1/_{32}$ cup or $^1/_3$ oz.
3 tsp.	=	1 Tbls. or $^1/_{16}$ cup or $^1/_2$ oz.
6 tsp.	=	2 Tbls. or $^1/_8$ cup or 1 oz.
12 tsp.	=	4 Tbls. or $^1/_4$ cup or 2 oz.
16 tsp.	=	$5^1/_2$ Tbls. or $^1/_3$ cup or $2^2/_3$ oz.
24 tsp.	=	8 Tbls. or $^1/_2$ cup or 4 oz.
32 tsp.	=	$10^2/_3$ Tbls. or $^2/_3$ cup or $5^1/_3$ oz.
36 tsp.	=	12 Tbls. or $^3/_4$ cup or 6 oz.
48 tsp.	=	16 Tbls. or 1 cup or 8 oz.
1 cup	=	$^1/_2$ pt. or $^1/_4$ qt. or $^1/_{16}$ gal. or 8 oz.
2 cups	=	1 pt. or $^1/_2$ qt. or $^1/_8$ gal. or 16 oz.
3 cups	=	$1^1/_2$ pt. or $^3/_4$ qt. or $^3/_{16}$ gal. or 24 oz.
4 cups	=	2 pt. or 1 qt. or $^1/_4$ gal. or 32 oz.
5 cups	=	$2^1/_2$ pt. or $1^1/_4$ qt. or $^5/_{16}$ gal. or 40 oz.
6 cups	=	3 pt. or $1^1/_2$ qt. or $^3/_8$ gal. or 48 oz.
8 cups	=	4 pt. or 2 qt. or $^1/_2$ gal. or 64 oz.
10 cups	=	5 pt. or $2^1/_2$ qt. or $^5/_8$ gal. or 80 oz.
12 cups	=	6 pt. or 3 qt. or $^3/_4$ gal. or 96 oz.
16 cups	=	8 pt. or 4 qt. or 1 gal. or 128 oz.

INDEX